INCREDIBLE
FLYING
MACHINES

INCREDIBLE
FLYING
MACHINES

An anthology of eccentric aircraft

Michael F. Jerram

Exeter Books

NEW YORK

Marshall Cavendish
London & Sydney

Front endpapers : The fascinating Convair XFY-1 'Pogo' was designed in the early 1950s as part of a programme to provide the US Navy with a VTOL fighter. The 'Pogo' was intended to take off and land vertically, transitioning to and from forward flight in the air.

Back endpapers : The Short-Mayo Composite was a 1930s attempt to secure long range for mailplanes with the aid of a piggy-back arrangement. The Composite took off on the power of all eight engines, and when sufficient altitude had been gained, the 'Maia' mother craft released the 'Mercury' floatplane for a high-speed dash.

Title page : The extra-ordinary Gossamer Albatross took the world by considerable surprise when it achieved the first man-powered crossing of the English Channel in 1979.

This page : One of the more daring spirits in the 1930s was Jimmie Goodwin, an American daredevil who 'flew' with the aid of vanes.

Overleaf : One of the fascinating designs originating from the drawing board of the prolific designer Burt Rutan, the Vari-Viggen is a compact canard lightplane of good performance.

Prepared by
Talos Publishing Limited,
31/9 Chenies Street,
London WC1E 7ET.

Editor: Chris Chant
Picture researcher: John Moore
Designer: Bob Burroughs

Published and distributed by:

Marshall Cavendish Books Limited
58 Old Compton Street
London W1V 5PA

Exeter Books
Distributed by Bookthrift, Inc.
New York, New York

IN THE U.K., COMMONWEALTH AND REST OF THE WORLD, EXCEPT NORTH AMERICA

IN THE UNITED STATES OF AMERICA

ISBN 0 85685 835 8

ISBN 0-89673-072-7

INTRODUCTION

That birds can fly and men cannot seems too obvious to be worth stating, but it is a truism that many men have gallantly ignored. The birds' view of their imitators may never be known, but here is a book which puts the case for 'Those Magnificent Men' fairly and squarely. Aeroplanes stand for timetables, airport lounges and scheduled flights; flying machines for ingenuity, dreams and a prayer. With an aeroplane you take a ticket, with a flying machine you take a chance.

Man's ambition to fly admits of no logical chronology, and if Icarus was the first to try waxen wings he was doubtless not the last. Leonardo da Vinci took time off from his frescoes to assert that 'your flying machine ought not to imitate anything but the bat,' but was himself wise enough not to imitate his model with a night flight – and indeed never flew at all. Those quintessentially American Americans Orville and Wilbur Wright finally got aviation as we know it off the ground, but both before and since their historic ascent of 1903, man-powered flight has appealed to the pioneer designer.

If some of their schemes seem hare-brained now, this was not always so, and many of the 'contraptions' in this book were created in response to very real needs in the serious business of civil and military aviation. Since the achievement of the Wright brothers, the basic concept of heavier-than-air craft has been fixed within certain limits, but the visionaries have put forward some wonderful alternatives: tail-first aircraft with bizarre handling characteristics; aircraft that can be taken onto the road, and road cars which can be flown; aircraft which pack in a suitcase; aircraft for home construction, even flying saucers that actually fly.

Incredible Flying Machines is a tribute not only to the weird and wonderful aircraft, but also to the human beings – breaking legs far more often than records – who created them. It commemorates such maverick personalities as W. G. Tarrant whose one and only product was as high as a four-storey house and nose-dived into the ground prior to its only attempted flight and Doug 'Wrong-Way' Corrigan, who left New York bound for California and landed in Dublin blissfully unaware that he had crossed the Atlantic.

Some flying machines have proved so superior to the conventions of flight that it is strange how little the aeronautical establishment has been influenced; and indeed all flying machines deserve far greater credit and attention than they have hitherto received. The range is immense – from the world's smallest aircraft, the Stits Sky Baby, to Howard Hughes' gigantic Spruce Goose, with a multitude of visions and concepts in between. Since Icarus, the 'Magnificent Men' have come a long way, and will certainly go further still. But that is the beauty of flying machines – the sky is the limit.

CONTENTS

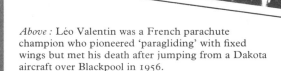

Chapter 1
MAKE LIKE A BIRD

Envy of the birds' freedom of the air is one of man's oldest and most cherished dreams. Over the centuries it has inspired men to emulate the feathered tribe – or rather to make the attempt, for no one has yet succeeded fully. The idea of merely copying the birds with a pair of extemporized but wholly ineffective 'wings' begins with the fable of Daedalus and Icarus, and proceeds with a tragi-comical mixture of laughter and disaster through numerous birdman efforts of the dark and medieval ages; only with the coming of the age of reason does a more sensible approach appear, leading via the work of Lilienthal to the current 'golden age' of hang-gliding.

Above : Léo Valentin was a French parachute champion who pioneered 'paragliding' with fixed wings but met his death after jumping from a Dakota aircraft over Blackpool in 1956.

Left : The cheapest and perhaps the most exciting way to get into the air is with a hang-glider. Such aircraft, which re-entered the aviation scene in the 1970s, take the pilot right back to the days of Otto Lilienthal, but with the added safety of modern materials.

BIRD-ENVY, THOUGH not the oldest of man's vices, is surely one of the longest lived. It dates from prehistory, when cave-dwellers bent upon self-preservation and survival in a hostile environment undoubtedly coveted the ease with which flying creatures could escape a predator with the beat of a wing.

As every first-year student of Greek mythology knows, the first humans to match the birds at their own game were Daedalus and Icarus, a father-and-son formation who soared away from captivity on King Minos's island of Crete on wings fashioned from linen, feathers and wax. Icarus' wings came unglued at the zenith of his climb and he crashed fatally into the sea, achieving distinction as the world's first recorded air accident victim, if you care to believe this improbable tale. But even if he did exist, Icarus was but the first of a persistent, misguided multitude to litter the long, hard path to human flight with shattered limbs and scattered feathers.

Equally doubtful is the tale of an ancient British birdman, King Bladud, who supposedly assumed the throne of Britain in 863 B.C., having first founded the city of Bath and created its therapeutic spa waters with his magical powers, and who is said to have attempted to establish his greatness by flying from the Temple of Apollo in Trinaventum, now the city of London. Alas the poor monarch's *magicke* let him down, quite literally.

Far from being cautionary, such myths inspired many other would-be birdmen, though not all were willing fliers. At Roman games prisoners were sometimes made to soar into arenas full of wild animals on makeshift wings, while other enforced 'flights' were made in the name of sacrifice.

From heaven to earth
For long centuries flight remained the realm of divine beings, or those who aspired to godliness, like Eilmer, a Benedictine monk who fitted himself out with a pair of wings and launched himself forth from the abbey at Malmesbury in Wiltshire, some 32 km (20 miles) from King Bladud's magnificent Bath. John Milton wrote of Eilmer in 1670 that 'he flew more than a Furlong; but the wind being too high, came fluttering down,

The first printed representation of flight appeared in 1493, in the form of a woodcut entitled 'The Flight of Daedalus and the Fall of Icarus' in Riederer's *Spiegel der Wahren Rhetoric*: Daedalus looks on with anxiety as Icarus plummets towards the water shedding feathers. It also appears that Icarus has been preceded by an example of the genuine feathered tribe.

to the maiming of all his limbs; yet so conceited in his Art, that he attributed the cause of his fall to the want of a Tail, as Birds have, which he forgot to make to his hinder parts.'

A stained-glass window in Malmesbury Abbey depicts the tailless Eilmer, a pair of pitifully inadequate wings strapped to his chest, and a bar in the town is named *The Flying Monk* in tribute to this 'first man to have flown in Europe', albeit briefly and painfully.

Tower-jumping peaked (numerically, if not in achievement) between the sixteenth and eighteenth centuries, when any number of fledgling birdmen hurled themselves aloft. As often as not they were clerical gentlemen, who saw in their crude wings the key to the doors of heaven. And as often as not they were right. John Wilkins, Bishop of Chester, made a study of their activities, and wrote a treatise upon them in *Mathematical Magicke*, published in 1648.

'There are four severall ways whereby this flying in the air has been or may be attempted,' he vouched. 'Two of them by the strength of other things, and two of them by our owne strength. 1. By Spirits or Angels. 2. By the help of Fowls. 3. By Wings fastened immediately to the body. 4. By Flying Chariot.'

Wilkins placed most faith in his flying chariots, which he accurately predicted 'would be serviceable also for the conveyance of a man to any remote place on this earth', but he also allowed that 'Tis the more obvious and common opinion that this [flying] may be effected by wings fastened immediately to the body, this coming nearest to the imitation of nature.'

Rise and fall

It was the slavish imitation of nature, in the form of attempts to emulate the birds, which was to delay man's flight centuries beyond the discovery and perfection of more demanding sciences. One of those who apparently achieved a measure of success was an Italian mathematician called Giovanni Baptiste Danti. This 'Daedalus of Perugia' donned a pair of iron-stayed wings and is said to have made flights across Lake Trasimeno around A.D. 1498. A fellow Perugian, Cesare Alessi, reported Danti's rise and eventual fall in 1652:

'Having arranged these [his wings] so as to produce an effective flight he several times tried them over Lake Trasimeno. As soon as they responded perfectly to his control, he decided to try them publicly in Perugia. And when in that town a great gathering of eminent people was assembled for the nuptials of the sister of Giampaolo Baglioni . . . and when a great crowd of people were gathered in the great square for jousting, behold, suddenly there was Danti, flying through the air from a high part of our city with a great rushing sound, enveloped in various kinds of feathers, crossing from one side to the other of the square with his great pair of wings, so astonishing everyone, and indeed terrifying quite a few, that they thought they were witness to some great and portentous monster. But when, having left the low earth behind, he was trying with his proud limbs to attain through the high air the summit of his genius, envious Fortune, indignant at so much audacity, broke the iron bar which controlled the left wing, and as Danti could not sustain the weight of his body with the help of the other wing alone, he fell heavily on to the roof of the church of St. Mary, and to his great distress, and that of everyone, hurt his leg.'

Danti never tempted the envious Fortune again. He hung up his wings and abandoned the precarious business of display flying for the comfortably precise science of mathematics, made all the more comfortable by a generous stipend from Giampaolo Baglioni, whose sister's wedding he had so enlivened.

Danti died from a fever at the age of 40, making his last, heaven-bound flight 'on the wings of his virtue more safely than he had flown on counterfeit wings while living,' according to Alessi.

A fellow-countryman of Danti, by name John Damian, knew a thing or two about counterfeit wings. He was a confidence trickster, a 'milker of purses', who fled Italy and France in the wake of some devious frauds and arrived in Scotland in 1501, where he quickly found favour with King James IV. The gullible king enjoyed Damian's 'merry nature', and appointed him Abbot of Tungland in 1504 in recognition of his (non-existent) powers as an alchemist and surgeon. The king's courtiers were less easily taken in and to a man distrusted Damian. Unable to win them over with his alchemy, Damian mounted the battlements of Stirling Castle on 27 September 1507, thence to fly to Paris to arrive ahead of ambassadors despatched overland by James IV. His journey was indeed swift . . . and vertical. But even as he climbed ignominiously from the dunghill in which he had landed the smooth-talking shyster had a ready explanation. 'My wings', he told the king, 'were composed of various feathers. Among them were the feathers of a dunghill fowl, and they, by a certain sympathy, were attracted to the dunghill on which I fell; whereas, had my wings been composed of eagles alone, as I proposed, the same sympathy would have attracted my machine to the higher regions of the air.'

The age of reason

Among a flurry of birdmen who flapped their way awkwardly from rooftops in the seventeenth and eighteenth centuries were a

Above : One of the many fanciful depictions of Besnier's 'flight' at Sablé in 1678 shows the daring inventor using his hinged flappers, which might have been just enough to break his fall when he 'soared over a house and landed safely'.

Right : A latter-day realization reveals the basic soundness of Sir George Cayley's 1852 design for a fixed-wing glider with inherent longitudinal and lateral stability, control being effected by the movable cruciform tail surfaces. Despite its prophetic nature, the design went virtually unnoticed at the time.

trio of Frenchmen: a locksmith named Besnier; a nobleman, the Marquis de Bacqueville; and a former army general, Resnier de Goué.

Besnier is said to have made a successful flight at Sablé in 1678 using an 'Engine for Flying'. It comprised a pair of poles to the ends of which were attached taffeta-covered, oblong, hinged paddles or vanes, the poles being balanced on Besnier's shoulders and connected by strings to his ankles, so that the flying action was something akin to swimming and canoeing at the same time, and about as effective. On the downstrokes the vanes opened up to scoop in air; on the upstrokes they closed to lessen resistance. Curiously, illustrations of the apparatus usually show the locksmith entirely naked – as a weight-saving ploy, perhaps? The vanes of Besnier's craft appear too small to have acted even as a rudimentary parachute, far less to have enabled him to go flitting around rooftops. None the less, he stirred public imagination as well as air with his paddles, and had sense enough to quit while he was ahead, or at least alive, selling off his 'engine' to a travelling showman.

De Bacqueville was an eccentric, given to 'extravagant tastes and wild opinions'. One such opinion was that he could fly. At the age of 62 he should have known better. Perhaps at heart he did, for the marquis first ordered his valet to try out the wings which he had devised for his arms and legs. Servants seem often to have been employed against their wills as test pilots by noblemen dabbling in aeronautics, most notably by the great British pioneer Sir George Cayley, whose coachman resigned after crashing in one of his master's creations. De Bacqueville's man would have none of it. 'Monsieur le Marquis,' pleaded the wily flunkey, 'a valet cannot precede his master.' Proper etiquette (and the valet's skin) thus preserved, de Bacqueville had no option but to

take wing himself, launching out from a top window of his home on the Rue des Saintes-Pères on what is now the Quai Voltaire in Paris in 1742. He flailed wildly in an effort to cross the River Seine to the Tuileries Gardens before a tub of dirty linen in a passing washerwoman's barge broke his fall and his legs.

General de Goué was even older, but little wiser, than de Bacqueville. In 1801, at the age of 72, the old soldier plunged off the ramparts of Angoulême, straight into the River Charente. Undeterred, he repeated the effort over dry land, the result being the almost inevitable broken legs.

The scientific revolution?

With the coming of the nineteenth century and the industrial revolution, many would-be fliers turned to more elaborate, though scarcely more successful flying machines. Jean-Marie Le Bris, an old sea-dog who had studied the behaviour of the albatross on his many voyages, constructed a man-carrying replica of the bird. Sitting in its boat-shaped body he could alter the angle of incidence of its 15.25-m (50-ft) wings with a pair of oar-like levers attached to the main spars, so that he looked like the master of some peculiar aerial rowing-boat.

Le Bris had his machine mounted on a cart which was towed into stiff breezes on the beach at Douarnenez by a horse in the late 1850s. As the animal broke into a trot the albatross kited up on the wind to an altitude of 100 m (328 ft), whereupon the tow-rope entwined itself around the neck of the accompanying coachman (another one!) and hauled him up, too. Fortunately the horse pulled up, and coachman, sea-dog and machine were deposited in the sand. If the coachman had been wise, he would have handed in his notice there and then, like Cayley's did.

The wings of Le Bris's machine did not flap, like those of its namesake, but elsewhere in Europe inventive birdmen were working on ornithopters, or flapping-wing craft. In Vienna a Swiss clockmaker named Jacob Degen fashioned a *Flugmaschine* of this kind, but static tests revealed his muscles capable of producing just 25 kg (55 lb) of lift. Machine and man weighed four times that, so Degen suspended it beneath a small hydrogen balloon and was soon being acclaimed as the first man to fly under his own power. He was quick to point out that the balloon was there purely for 'stability', and when contemporary illustrators showed his machine devoid of the vital gasbag, Degen did nothing to discourage the notion that he was indeed flying by his own strength. But when he brought the machine to Paris in 1812 for a series of exhibition flights, strong winds soon carried balloon, ornithopter and 'pilot' away, and the disappointed Parisian crowd, realizing that they had been fooled, attacked the charlatan, destroyed his machine and drove him out of town.

The deceptive reports of Degen's 'flights' inspired imitators, among them Albrecht Berblinger, a tailor who leaped from the Adlerbastei at Ulm in 1811. Contemporary illustrations show the unfortunate tailor splashing around in the River Danube while onlookers watch with ill-concealed delight.

The ornithopter proved also to be the downfall of Vincent de Groof. He was a Belgian cobbler who built a kind of parachute-cum-ornithopter. Banned by the authorities from attempting to fly in his native land, de Groof came to England in the summer of 1874 and made a successful descent from beneath a balloon over Epping Forest on 29 June. A week later he ascended under the balloon to 305 m (1000 ft) over the River Thames, cut loose and immediately plunged into a Chelsea street and was killed when his flapper's wings failed under air load. 'Such deplorable events as this serve to prove once more that the path of the inventor is indeed strewn with thorns,' *The Times* noted sagely next day, as if anyone needed reminding.

Lilienthal: the true dawn

In Germany, meanwhile, a young man named Otto Lilienthal was making an intensive study of bird anatomy and flying characteristics, inspired by the storks which he and his brother Gustav watched wheeling over the rooftops of Potsdam, their home town. Not for Otto the mere fundamentals with which so many of his predecessors had been content: he sought to discover precisely how birds flew, altering the dihedral angle of their wings for lateral stability, and varying the camber of the surfaces for lift or drag. Lilienthal was quick to appreciate the importance of curved wing surfaces. In 1889 he published the results of his findings in his book *Der Vogelflug als Grundlage der Fliegekunst* (Bird Flight as the Basis of the Flying Art), and

set about testing his theories.

Two years later Lilienthal completed a monoplane glider constructed from peeled willow wands with a covering of waxed cotton. Its wings spanned 7 m (23 ft), with Lilienthal supporting himself within its centre section on parallel bars – literally a hang-glider – and controlling his flight path by shifting his body mass and thus altering the craft's centre of gravity.

Lilienthal's first tentative hops were made with the aid of a springboard launcher, but soon he gained confidence enough to fly from a specially constructed 15-m (49-ft) hill on the outskirts of Berlin.

In five years Otto constructed seven gliders (five monoplanes and two biplanes) and made over 2000 ever-improving flights from hill sites at Stieglitz and in the Rhinow Mountains near Stöllen. He flew distances up to 400 m (1312 ft) and reached heights of 25 m (82 ft). More than that, he discovered and made use of upcurrents of air for soaring flight. Here he describes his take-off technique: 'With folded wings you run against the wind and off the mountain, at the appropriate moment turning the bearing surface of the wings slightly upwards so that it is almost horizontal. Now, hovering in the wind, you try to put the apparatus into such a position in relation to the centre of gravity that it shoots rapidly away and drops as little as possible. The essential thing is the proper regulation of the centre of gravity; he who will fly must be just as much the master of this as a cyclist is of his balance.'

This is the classic hang-gliding technique, as relevant today as it was when freshly discovered a century ago. Within those five years Lilienthal's courageous research achieved more than all the tower jumpers and flappers had in 2000 years or more. He might well have gone on to even greater achievements (powerplants for his gliders were to have been his next step) but on the evening of 9 August 1896, Otto was at Stöllen testing a new kind of head-movement control arrangement when a sudden gust upturned his glider and he crashed heavily from 15 m (49 ft) breaking

After extensive experiments with monoplane hang-gliders, the German pioneer Otto Lilienthal in 1895 produced his thirteenth design, a neat biplane which was capable of relatively good soaring flights. The prospect of full control with moving surfaces, rather than by movement of the pilot's body, had long attracted Lilienthal, as had the prospect of powered flight: but on 9 August 1896 Lilienthal crashed after a stall in his *No. 11* monoplane, and died on the following day before he could progress further with his experiments.

Above : A 1930s rival of Jimmie Goodwin was a fellow American, Clem Sohn, seen here before a 'flight' at Vincennes in 1937.

Right : The annual birdman contest off a pier in the British resort town of Bognor Regis attracts large numbers of entries, some of them relatively serious and others of them undeniably flippant. Seen here is one of the more ambitious entries for the glide distance which has yet to be achieved.

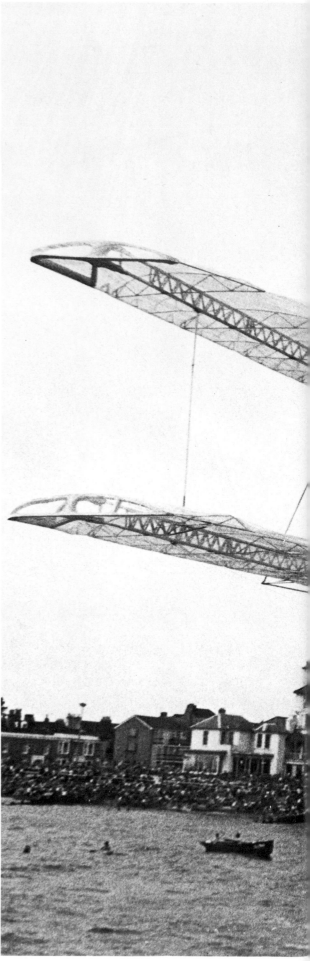

his spine. 'Sacrifices must be made,' he remarked resignedly, and died next day from his injuries.

Within a decade of Otto Lilienthal's death, however, the dream of bird-like flight, so agonizingly long in realization, had all but been forgotten for the promise of the internal combustion engine.

Backward steps

Yet the birdman notion persisted, first as an airshow curiosity when men like Jimmie Goodwin, Clem Sohn and Léo Valentin fleshed out the Superman cartoons with canvas wings and iron courage, and lately in the sport of hang-gliding. You too can be an Icarus (or better still a Daedalus) for the price of a Rogallo kite.

And, incredibly in the hard-nosed face of late twentieth-century aerospace technology, the fabulous, futile flappers are still with us. In a Staten Island workshop Professor James FitzPatrick works away perfecting his Mark CCCXX (320) ornithopter, the basic type with which he has been concerned for these past 45 years. 'Modern airplanes fly with all the efficiency of a barn door,' FitzPatrick asserts optimistically as his absurd pterodactyl hisses, heaves and clanks, compressed air muscles beating its wings up and down once a second. It moves not one inch, but FitzPatrick has The Faith: one day his ornithopter will flap away to join in spirit with the 200-odd birds he dissected to perfect his mechanisms.

Perhaps the birdman syndrome is best summed up by a cartoon published in an American magazine. At the edge of a cliff stands a man with feathery wings outstretched. Behind him an anxious-looking wife is saying: 'Now, dear, let's see if I have this right. If you crash, who is it I contact, the Federal Aviation Administration or the National Audubon Society?'

Chapter 2
PUFFED UP

The first successful balloon flight in 1783 was succeeded by an era of 'balloonacy' as men realized that flight of a kind was possible, and tried in all manner of ways to turn the free-floating balloon into a practical method of mass transportation. Grandiose schemes abounded, to the delight of the public, but it was not until the second half of the nineteenth century that the dirigible airship became a practical flying machine, thanks to the efforts of Santos Dumont and the Graf von Zeppelin. But the era of the dirigible was short, and the few current airships are little more than curiosities for advertising purposes.

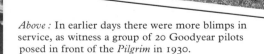

Above : In earlier days there were more blimps in service, as witness a group of 20 Goodyear pilots posed in front of the *Pilgrim* in 1930.

Left : The Goodyear non-rigid airship *Mayflower* moves in stately grace over the spectator fleet following one of the races for the America's Cup off Newport, Rhode Island. The *Mayflower* was completed in 1976, and is smaller than the three other Goodyear blimps currently in service: she is filled with helium, and on each side are illuminated panels for advertising purposes.

O NE OF THE curious facts of aviation
history is that more than a century
before man finally found a pair of
wings to bear him aloft, hot air was
doing just that, and balloonists were actually
making aerial journeys while the flappers
were still floundering and breaking their
limbs.

Joseph and Etienne Montgolfier are
credited with the invention of the balloon in
1783 – inspired by a notion to 'capture a
cloud in a bag' and soar up on it – but there
is some circumstantial evidence that inhabi-
tants of southern Peru might have flown in
hot-air balloons 2000 years ago. A balloon
design has been discovered on pre-Inca
pottery and students of ancient Peruvian
history believe that the Nazcas, a coastal
race who inhabited southern Peru from
100 B.C. to A.D. 700, may have fashioned
balloons from cotton and reed, both of them
freely available during that time.

A British balloonist has constructed a
replica of the pottery design balloon and
flown it successfully over the Plain of Nazca
on the Peruvian/Bolivian border where a
520 sq km (200 sq mile) area of desert is
covered with ancient markings and drawings: arrow-straight lines just a few metres
wide which stretch for 16 km (10 miles)
with almost unbelievable precision; tri-
angles and rectangles 1½ km (1 mile) long;
and vast, exquisite drawings of birds, fish
and animals. These pose the tantalizing
question why (and how) did this primitive
race create such immense, elaborate and
geometrically precise designs when they
could not see the results, for *Las Lineas* are
quite invisible from the ground; Perhaps
they were indeed able to fly.

The world's first 'balloonists', Nazcas
aside, were a cockerel, a duck and a sheep
which ascended in Etienne de Montgolfier's *Martial* balloon from a courtyard at
the Palace of Versailles on 19 September
1783 in the presence of King Louis XVI.
The poor cock was also ballooning's first
victim, for it broke its neck on landing. The
sheep lived to become an honoured curiosity
in Marie Antoinette's private zoo.

The first manned flight took place a
month later, on 15 October 1783, when a
young naturalist named Jean-François
Pilâtre de Rozier stayed aloft for four
minutes on the end of a 15-m (50-ft) rope,
following that with an 8-km (5-mile) free
flight across Paris with the Marquis
d'Arlandes as a passenger on 21 November.
The balloon must have made a magnificent
sight, its lemon-shaped bag decorated with
gold fleurs-de-lis, signs of the zodiac and
Louis XVI's royal monogram. It was the
Montgolfiers' intention to crew it with con-
demned criminals, who were expendable
anyway, but Pilâtre de Rozier pleaded that

Right : The imagination of
many Frenchmen ran riot
during the heady days of the
Napoleonic Wars, as witness
this fantastic notion for an
airborne invasion of England
by a vast army transported
across the English Channel in
hot-air balloons. In this page
from the *Publiciste* of May
1803 (specifically 13 Prairial
de l'An XI), it was claimed
that some 3,000 men could be
carried by each of the balloons,
which would each cost only
300,000 francs.

Below : A contemporary
depiction of the Montgolfier
balloon in which Pilâtre de
Rozier and the Marquis de
l'Arlandes made the world's
first manned flight on 15
October 1783 gives an
indication of the balloon's
grandeur, vividly described
in the text accompanying the
illustration.

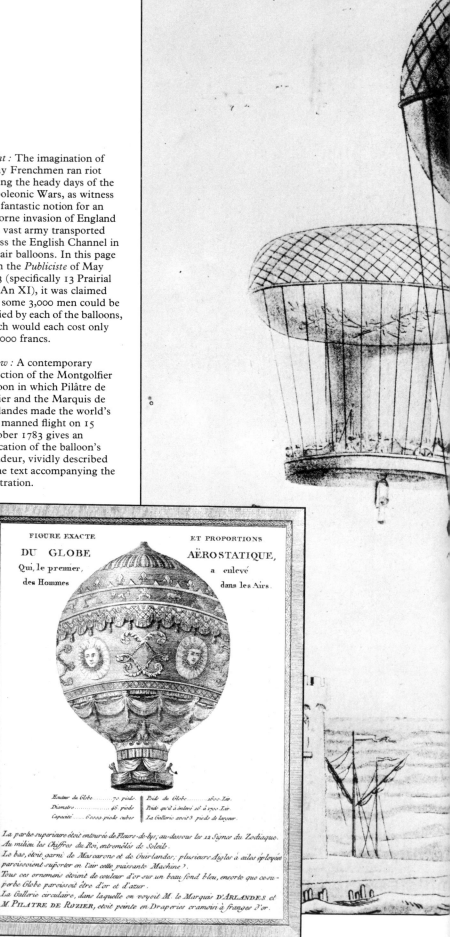

FIGURE EXACTE   ET PROPORTIONS
DU GLOBE   AËROSTATIQUE,
Qui, le premier,
des Hommes   a enlevé
           dans les Airs.

Hauteur du Globe...........70 pieds. | Poids du Globe...........1600 Liv.
Diametre.................46 pieds | Poids qu'il a enlevé 16 à 1700 Liv.
Capacité...........60000 pieds cubes | La Gallerie avoit 3 pieds de largeur.

*La partie superieure étoit entourée de Fleurs-de-lys; au-dessous les 12 Signes du Zodiaque.
Au milieu les Chiffres du Roi, entremêlés de Soleils.
Le bas, étoit garni de Mascarons et de Guirlandes; plusieurs Aigles à ailes éployées
paroissoient suporter en l'air cette puissante Machine .
Tous ces ornemens étoient de couleur d'or sur un beau fond bleu, ensorte que ce su-
perbe Globe paroissoit être d'or et d'azur .
La Gallerie circulaire, dans laquelle on voyoit M. le Marquis D'ARLANDES et
M. PILATRE DE ROZIER, étoit peinte en Draperies cramoisi à franges d'or.*

the honour should go to someone more worthy: 'Shall vile criminals, foul murderers, men rejected from the bosom of society, have the glory of being first to navigate the field of air?' he asked, not unreasonably. Pilâtre de Rozier died in a ballooning accident on 15 June 1785, while attempting to cross the English Channel from France to England, six months after a successful crossing had been made in the other direction.

'Balloonacy'

The years following that first balloon ascent were heady indeed. Europe went balloon mad. Ladies' fashions took on a balloon look: 'aerostats', as they were called, appeared on vases and crockery, and one enterprising French publicist built a 5-m ($16\frac{1}{2}$-ft) high mannequin called the Aerostatic Grape Picker which was launched from the Tuileries in Paris and went floating away over the countryside causing no small panic among the populace.

The possibilities opened up by aerostation seemed limitless. A Spaniard envisioned aerial bullfights, with snorting toro and mounted picador suspended from captive balloons. The bullfighter's balloon could be moved relative to his stationary quarry by means of a guide rope, so that the animal would have stood no chance had anyone been foolish enough to try it. A year after the Montgolfier triumph a Frenchman named Saint-Just thought he could improve on their globular balloon; aerostats, he thought, should be shaped as fish, with the fins, scales and all. His 1784 St Just *Flying Fish* had no means of taking off or landing. 'My first concern', he declared, 'is to make it fly. The minor problems may be solved later.'

Even odder was the 'grand Aerostatic Machine and Sailing Apparatus, consisting of means of Directing, Depressing and Raising it at Pleasure' devised by a Mr Prosser in England. This was a fantastic balloon in the shape of a caricature of Sir John Falstaff. It was to have been 11 m (36 ft) high with a girth around Sir John's ample waist of 21 m (69 ft), and would have been propelled by a sail and oars – totally ineffective since the speed of a free balloon relative to the surrounding air is always zero.

The search for greater and greater absurdity proceeded apace. On 16 October 1798 Pierre Testu-Brissy made the first-ever equestrian balloon ascent at Bellevue, his mount standing on a specially constructed platform beneath the gasbag. Perhaps this event inspired a mad proposal put forward to Napoleon Bonaparte for an airborne invasion of Britain. The idea was that massive 'montgolfiers' (the French still call hot-air balloons 'montgolfiers' to this day) would cross the Channel, each carrying as many as 6000 cavalry.

No more practical, though magnificently eccentric, was the *Minerva* balloon of Flemish physicist Etienne Gaspard Robertson: 'an aerial ship designed for exploration and offered to all the Academies of Europe' – a magnanimous gesture indeed. Robertson thought his 46-m (150-ft) balloon 'would be of immense use in the science of geography, and when under the line (equator), if the heat near the earth be inconvenient the aeronauts would easily rise to elevations where the temperature is equal and agreeable. When their observations, their needs or their pleasures demanded it, they could descend to within a short distance of the earth, say 90 ft [27 m], and fix themselves in their position by means of an anchor. It might be possible by taking advantage of favourable winds to make the tour of the world.'

What a voyage it might have been, for *Minerva*'s specification included an observatory; church; sports hall reserved for recreation, walking and gymnastics; lecture hall for scientific conferences; chemistry laboratory; large store to keep 'water, wine and all nutritive substances for the expedition'; a kitchen; musical activities room; carpentry workshop; iron foundry; laundry; private studies; and, best of all, 'quarters for a few interested ladies, this part set at a distance from the body of the construction, lest the learned travellers be distracted in their observations'! There was also to be a small ship on which to sail home 'should the balloon be in a state of decay', and a smaller balloon to be used as a tender. On top of *Minerva*'s Lyons silk envelope was a large cockerel at whose eyes telescopes were mounted for observing earth or heavens. 'Each aeronaut [*Minerva* was to have carried 60] will be obliged to carry a parachute on his person throughout the journey,' Robertson cautioned, even in the company of those 'interested ladies', one imagines. Needless to say, the *Minerva* was never built.

To steer a balloon
The problem with balloons is that they are entirely at the mercy and whim of wind. In 1785 a Frenchman suggested an 'infallible method for controlling balloons' which involved tying them to a pair of donkeys, the whole contraption then being driven along like an aerial stage-coach; another sage thought that tethered birds might do a better job. These were not to be just any birds, moreover, but specially trained eagles, though he allowed that 'perhaps strong pigeons might do' provided one carried a spare brace for when the first birds tired!

The search for a navigable balloon, free from capricious winds, was studded with bold and imaginative ideas but little actual hardware. Among early dirigibles was the *Dolphin* of 1816 designed by Samuel Pauley, a Swiss engineer living in London, and his fellow countryman Durs Egg who was Royal Gunsmith to King George III of England. The fish-shaped *Dolphin* was 27 m (90 ft) long and made of goldbeater's skin – the gas-tight intestine on an ox – stretched over a wooden frame. Movable fins and oars were supposed to propel it through the air, while an adjustable weight on a pulley served to balance it fore and aft. Pauley died before the ship could be flown, and Egg abandoned his 'folly', as fellow Knightsbridge residents dubbed the flying fish.

'The Eagle, First Aerial Ship' proclaimed posters in London in 1835. 'The First Experiment of this New System of Aerial Navigation will sail from Victoria Road, Kensington early in August, with government dispatches and passengers for Paris... on its future voyages it will sail for Vienna, Berlin, Petersburgh and other Principal Cities on the Continent.'

Eagle was a creation of the Comte de Lennox, a Scotsman who served with the French Army. In the previous year his first airship had been torn to shreds by an angry crowd of Parisians when it failed to make a much-publicized flight from the Champ de Mars. *Eagle,* manned by 17 'experimental sailors', was propelled by paddles and would reach Paris in six hours carrying passengers who would 'be admitted to share the pleasures of the voyage at a reasonable rate,' Lennox declared. However, he soon found that by charging one shilling admission (two guineas for a whole year's privileges) to view *Eagle* at the self-styled European Aeronautical Society's 'dockyard' near Kensington Gardens, he could get rich without risk, and the aerial ship remained nothing more than a sightseeing curiosity.

Transcontinental transport
Handbills appearing on the streets of New York in the winter of 1848 promised even greater things than Lennox had. 'Best Route to California', they proclaimed, 'New York to California in three days, fully demonstrated ... A perfect Aerial Locomotive [which] will have a capacity to carry from 50 to 100 passengers at a speed of 60 to 100 miles per hour [97 to 161 kph]. It is expected to put this machine in operation about the 1st of April 1849. It is proposed to carry a limited number of passengers – not exceeding 300 – for $50, including board, and the transport is expected to make a trip to the gold region and back in seven days. The price of passage to California is fixed at

'Balloonomania' was virtually endemic in Europe after the first success of the Montgolfier brothers' paper creation. Typical of the more far-fetched ideas that abounded at the time were those for Boult's Flying Apartment House (*right*), an impossible proposition with a balloon at each end, a pusher propeller, and control effected by oars; the St. Just Flying Fish of 1783 which was to be made of tinplate, lifted by hydrogen, and both propelled and controlled with sprung taffeta fins in just the same way as a fish; and the Petin Flying Ship of 1850 (*below*), which comprised a timber frame lifted by four huge balloons, with inclined planes for control in climb and dive.

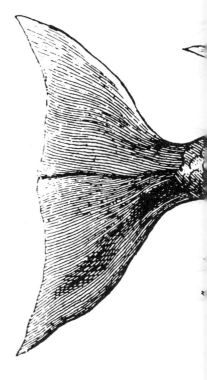

$200, with the exception above mentioned.'

The author was Rufus Porter, founder of *Scientific American* magazine, whose transcontinental 'aeroport' was to be 213 m (700 ft) long. He sold shares in it, each entitling the buyer to ownership of one three-thousandth part of the ship. The *Philadelphia Enquirer* cautioned readers to have none of it:

'It would seem as if the gullibility of human nature kept even pace with the wit of knaves, and that nothing could be proposed from an exhibition too preposterous to find believers . . . a flying machine can never be steered. Yet, as in the analogous instance of perpetual motion, there will be found dolts to believe in it, we suppose, to the end of time.'

Porter never did build his aerial locomotive, though he did manage a 49-m (160-ft) ship whose cloth covering rotted before it could be flown. His own publication *Scientific American* subsequently ridiculed a similar project from a Mr E. J. Pennington, of Mount Carmel, Illinois in 1891:

'In the popular belief the flying machine is next to an accomplished fact and no very great surprise probably would be occasioned if the announcement were made tomorrow morning that a line of airships had commenced to run between Chicago and New York. We are sorry, however, to be obliged to dash the hopes of a confiding public . . . our glorious people are likely to, for some time to come, be confined in their locomotion to the actual earth's surface. . . . Various schemes for air-flying look fine on paper. One of these paper enterprises is styled the Pennington Airship. Twenty millions of dollars is the modest amount of the capital. A few of the shares have been reserved for sale to a hungry public. Those who have a dangerous surplus of cash in hand can promptly reduce it by investment in this deceptive and visionary scheme.'

Pennington's scheme was no more deceptive than Porter's had been, which is not to say much. He planned a large aluminium airship with wings accommodating horizontal propellers which would aid its buoyancy, and a large propeller at the 'bow' for forward motion, all being turned by a three-cylinder gas engine via shafts and belts. A 9.1-m (30-ft) model powered by an electric motor flew successfully at a Chicago exhibition.

There were many other such schemes: some were honest, but many more were the work of charlatans cashing in on public gullibility. A French milliner named Ernest Petin managed to take time out from hat designing to create a 'multiple airliner' which consisted of four gas balloons joined together by a 'deck' or promenade around which travellers could stroll in flight. It was guided by four helical screws operated 'manually or by other means'. Petin actually

built the craft, but sadly underestimated the power needed, and abandoned the idea in the face of ridicule, for the public were sometimes as ready to pour scorn as money into such projects. Perhaps driven by derision, another Frenchman, Alfred Julius Boult, devised a flying apartment house set between two balloons in which he planned to get away from it all and escape the city crowds. A steam engine powered eight oars which were supposed to row the house through the air, *Tricoleur* fluttering from its rooftop.

The first successful airship

Other inventors settled for less fanciful airships and were more successful. Henri Giffard, a talented young man who had already invented a steam injector for steam engines, successfully flew a 44-m (144-ft) steam-powered dirigible from the Hippodrome in Paris on 24 September 1852. His ship flew at 10 kph (6 mph), too slow for its rudder to be fully effective, though he did manage to make small steering corrections. Giffard realized that a much larger airship would be needed to lift an engine capable of providing more speed. He built a new airship measuring 600 m (1970 ft) in length and with a capacity of 220,875 cubic metres (7,800,000 cubic feet), which would have been capable of lifting a 30.5-tonne (30-ton) steam engine; its immense gasbag was destroyed during a test inflation and shortage of funds prevented Giffard from starting again.

The brothers Albert and Gaston Tissandier flew a 1060-cubic metre (37,500-cubic foot) electric-powered dirigible several times in the second half of 1884, but again low airspeed denied them effective steering and they too were forced to give up, their money exhausted.

The amazing Santos Dumont

True dirigibility was not demonstrated until the turn of the century when a young South American living in Paris was struck by an affliction he called 'airitis'. His name was Alberto Santos Dumont, the son of a wealthy Brazilian coffee-planter. Having tried his hand at ballooning Santos longed for a machine with which he could truly conquer the air and navigate where he, rather than the wind, chose. 'To my immense astonishment, I learned that there were no steerable balloons – that there were only spherical balloons like those of . . . 1784!' he wrote, incredulously. In the circumstances, Santos Dumont came to the inevitable conclusion that he would have to build his own.

His first dirigible was 25 m (82½ ft) long and contained 180 cubic metres (6400 cubic feet) of explosive hydrogen gas beneath

Alberto Santos Dumont, an expatriate Brazilian living in Paris, was one of the key figures in the development of European aviation. He is seen here, in his normal dapper turn-out, in the gondola of his elegant *No. 14* airship of 1905. This airship was never flight-tested, but is of considerable importance as Santos's last airship, and the craft under which he tested the heavier-than-air machine in which he achieved the first aeroplane flights in Europe.

which he suspended a $3\frac{1}{2}$-hp petrol engine. The combination of explosive gas and inflammable petrol was hardly wise, his well-meaning friends pointed out, but Santos was determined. On 18 September 1898 he took off from the *jardin d'acclimatisation* in the Bois de Boulogne and promptly ended up in a clump of trees. Know-all bystanders had advised him to take-off downwind. Two days later he was back, this time rising effortlessly into wind to complete a figure of eight 400 m (1300 ft) above an astonished, cheering crowd. 'Le Petit Santos' – for he weighed just 49 kg (108 lb) – was an instant hero, and very nearly a dead one; during his descent the gasbag collapsed. Quick thinking and the help of some small boys who grabbed his airship's trail rope saved him.

Santos embarked on an ambitious development programme after this modest triumph, and soon became a familiar sight puttering over the Paris suburb of Neuilly-Saint James on his latest dirigible. In the summer of 1901 he made two attempts to win a 125,000-franc prize offered by Henri Deutsche de la Meurthe for a flight from the *parc d'aerostation* at St Cloud to the Eiffel Tower and back, a distance of about 12 km ($7\frac{1}{2}$ miles), in half an hour. The first began on 13 July. With a following wind Santos's *No. 5* dirigible was soon rounding the Eiffel Tower, but on his return trip the little airship could make no headway, the time limit elapsed and the engine stopped. Santos valved off hydrogen and settled into a large

chestnut tree in the grounds of Edmund de Rothschild's house. He was still sitting on a branch, eating breakfast, when worried rescuers discovered him.

During his second attempt, on 8 August, Santos again circled the Eiffel Tower but was foiled on the way back, crashing noisily and explosively on to the roof of an hotel at Trocadéro. Shaken and singed he climbed through an attic window and was held by the manager on suspicion of cat burglary.

Another dirigible was hastily constructed to replace the wrecked *No. 5*, and on 19 October 1901 Santos just succeeded in making the round trip within the specified 30 minutes. Typically philanthropic, he divided the prize between his workers and the Parisian poor, keeping not a centime for himself. Santos built 14 airships in all, of which his diminutive *No. 9* was the best-known and most successful. On this personal runabout he challenged a friend's after-dinner remark that his dirigibles were no more than 'scientific curiosities' by flying right into the heart of Paris, landing in the Avenue des Champs-Elysées and mooring it on the railings of his house on the corner of Rue Washington while he went inside for coffee. Thereafter Parisians became quite blasé about the sight of *No. 9* parked outside fashionable restaurants or in the grounds of the country houses of Santos's many friends.

Zeppelin

With the practicality of dirigibles proven beyond dispute, balloons all but disappeared, and few indeed were those who did not see airships as the aerial transports of the future. Three decades later, *Graf* Ferdinand von Zeppelin's sky-monsters seemed to have proved them right, and to have brought the dreams of Porter, Pennington and their contemporaries to life. 'A fabulous silvery fish, floating quietly in an ocean of air . . . a fairy-like apparition which seems to be coming from another world and returning there like a dream,' was how the redoubtable Zeppelin captain Doctor Hugo Eckener described his airships.

Graf Zeppelin, the only airship ever to fly around the world, was nearly 240 m (787 ft) long. Some 850,000 head of cattle donated skins to contain its 105,000 cubic metres (3,708,000 cubic feet) of hydrogen, and 36 crew were on hand to serve 20 passengers with fine Rhine wines from crystal glasses in a burgundy-carpeted dining room as the ship cruised down to Rio on its transatlantic run. *Hindenburg* was even bigger: 50 passengers, with a sealed smoking room in which to savour good cigars, and a specially-made lightweight cast-aluminium grand piano for entertainment. No wonder that lighter-than-air seemed the only way to go, for no winged aircraft have ever rivalled the

Left : The Zeppelin airship LZ7, named *Deutschland*, can fairly be claimed as the world's first real passenger aircraft. This airship first flew on 19 October 1910, and was placed in service by the Zeppelin operator DELAG after extensive testing. It crashed in a forest shortly after this, and was replaced by the LZ8, named *Ersatz Deutschland*.

Below : Typical of the Goodyear airships currently in service as advertising and promotional craft is the *America*. Note the panel of lights under the company's name and symbol, computer-controlled to light up the appropriate slogan.

big airships for comfort or endurance. Then came *Hindenburg*'s bitter, fiery loss at Lakehurst, New Jersey in May 1937, chilling in its split-second destructiveness even on the scratchy newsreel film which caught its horrific end. We may never know for certain if it was a bomb, a gas leak or some other factor which caused the crash, but those few seconds brought an end not just to *Hindenburg*, but to the era of commercial airships.

Today ballooning is back in favour as a sport. For the cost of a small car you can buy a hot-air balloon and fly it, silent save for the occasional roar of the propane burner which gives it life, over busy summer roads packed with motorists dashing headlong for the coast, while you sip your traditional balloonist's breakfast of champagne in the still morning air.

There are still airships, too. The Goodyear Tyre & Rubber Company operate four 'blimps', non-rigid airships or 'rubber cows' made of neoprene-coated dacron puffed out into an unflattering but comfortable fat sausage shape by just over 5665 cubic metres (200,000 cubic feet) of non-inflammable helium gas. Goodyear use them for publicity, giving rides to dealers, distri-

butors, employees, press people and public figures, and for flashing public-service messages along their rubbery flanks on a computer-controlled 'Super Skytacular' night sign whose 7560 red, blue, green and yellow lights can convey anything from 'Save Gas' and 'Happy New Year' to moving cartoon pictures.

For the future Goodyear envisage bigger airships, more massive even than Count von Zeppelin's, which will be equipped with helicopter-type rotors and conventional propellers to provide additional lift and forward movement. Such craft would be used as cargo carriers, with payloads of 152 tonnes (150 tons) or more, and could aid in reducing port congestion by loading ships away from docks like airborne cranes, or for transporting heavy equipment to offshore locations.

And even the centuries-old idea of special-shaped balloons, such as the Falstaff figure, has been revived as a marketing ploy. Providing they can contain the necessary hot air, balloons can be made almost any shape, and are: lamp bulbs, sparking plugs, beer mugs, paint cans and even a pair of jeans have added a new dimension to the term 'publicity puff'.

Chapter 3

DREAMS, SCHEMES & MIGHT HAVE BEENS

Failure to turn the dream of flight into reality was largely attributable, in the minds of the pioneers, to the lack of a suitable powerplant. But then the beginning of the eighteenth century introduced the steam engine – and immediately there began a rash of steam-powered monsters that stood not a chance of success, as finally confirmed by the advent of the internal combustion engine.

Above : The extraordinary Ader *Avion III* is here seen with its bat-like wings folded for storage.

Left : Henson's Aerial Steam Carriage was the first realistic passenger aircraft to be designed as such.

THE TURN OF the eighteenth century brought with it a new era in the protracted search for powered, heavier-than-air flight, spurred by an exciting new form of power: steam.

What plans were laid on the strength of hissing valves and rumbling boilers! Foremost among the planners of what Horace Walpole termed 'mechanic meteors' was a Somerset linen trader and self-taught engineer called William Samuel Henson, whose catholic inventions hitherto had ranged from a new kind of razor and a breech-loading cannon to a self-cleaning device for lavatory cisterns.

In 1842, with the aid of his friend John Stringfellow, Henson drew up plans for an Aerial Steam Carriage. It was the first powered aircraft design in history to adopt what we now regard as a conventional configuration: monoplane wings with cambered surfaces, a movable tail for steering, and a tricycle undercarriage with iron-rimmed wheels. A steam engine developing some 30 hp was to turn a pair of seven-bladed, 3-m (10-ft) diameter propellers. Pilot and passengers of the machine, which was named *Ariel*, were housed in a fuselage shaped like the prow of a ship.

Henson was soon approached by an ambitious young journalist named Frederick Marriott who became his publicity agent and fund raiser. Marriott's talents as a publicist would have made Madison Avenue envious: in no time the Aerial Transit Company had been set up as the world's first airline, promising aerial voyages to all countries of the world aboard a fleet of *Ariels*. Lavish colour engravings were made showing evocative scenes of *Ariels*, red ensigns fluttering at their mastheads, flying over London, the pyramids of Egypt and the Great Wall of China. One newspaper attributed these fanciful commands to an *Ariel*'s captain:

'Keep your eye on Malta and get the parcels ready. Waken the old lady in No. 7 and drop the Pacha of Egypt's despatches. Tie a weight to the Suez post bag or it will be blown into the Mediterranean. Tell the Bombay gent in No. 25 to have his parachute in readiness, tie his hat on, shut his mouth and keep a fast hold as it's blowing a stiff breeze. Keep a sharp look out for Pekin and get the Emperor of China's letter ready as we shall drop on his palace directly.'

The public, gullible souls, loved it and firmly believed that the age of air travel was at hand. In truth the splendid *Ariel* did not exist at all. On Stringfellow's advice Henson had first built in 1847 a 6.1-m (20-ft) span model of the Steam Carriage (which would have spanned 45.7 m (150 ft), but the weight of its steam engine prevented it from doing

Below : The steam-powered ornithopter designed by the Scottish engineer J. M. Kaufmann attracted great interest when shown in model form at the 1868 Crystal Palace Exhibition. Located in the nose of the aircraft and fitted with a large funnel, the steam engine was to have powered two large propulsive flappers (moving downwards and backwards for thrust) while the aircraft was supported in the air by quadruplane wings. The fate of the model was typical of contemporary efforts: it thrashed itself to pieces, and Kaufmann gave up his experiments.

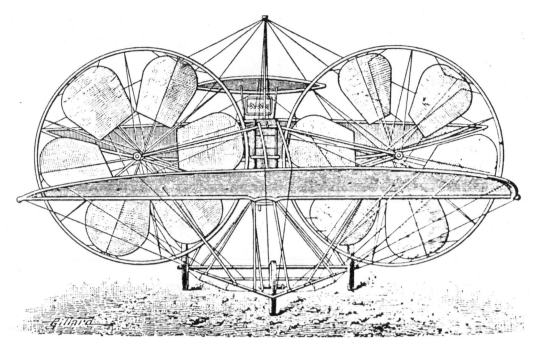

more than trundling off the end of its launching ramp. Discouraged and out of funds, Henson sought consolation in marriage and a new start in Texas. Marriott also went to America where he later proposed a transcontinental airline service using steam airliners which were part dirigible, part aeroplane. If nothing else, the *Ariel* was a prophetic design, and a triumph of mass-publicity. For decades afterwards reproductions of Marriott's engravings were popular and colourful wall decorations in English homes.

Félix du Temple, a French naval officer, in 1857 built a steam-powered model aircraft which could take-off and fly – hop, really – under its own power. Greatly encouraged he built a full-size machine which, for lack of a suitable powerplant, did not fly until 1874, when it too hopped into the air from a downhill run at Brest with a young sailor volunteer at the controls.

An extraordinary steamer was unveiled in model form at the 1868 Crystal Palace aeronautical exhibition, which was the world's first airshow. A Scots engineer from Glasgow proudly presented a steam-powered model ornithopter with fixed quadruplane wings, a pair of 'flappers' and a locomotive type body complete with funnel. J. M. Kaufmann seemingly planned to construct a full-size version of this romantic monstrosity, but was stopped short when the model thrashed itself to pieces on its first flapping-wing test.

In 1875 Thomas Moy had slightly more success at Crystal Palace with his Aerial Steamer, which had tandem wings and two immense paddle-bladed propellers driven by a 3-hp steam engine of his own design. Though unmanned, it managed to stagger 15 cm (6 in) above its circular test track on a tether, but was later damaged in a storm and quietly forgotten.

'The world's first flight' – again

Steaming through the air was not a notion entirely restricted to British and French inventors. An Imperial Russian Navy officer, Alexander Feodorovich Mozhaiski, is reported to 'have astounded St Petersburg' by flying a steam-powered machine in 1882 – two decades before the Wright Brothers first flew at Kitty Hawk. The claim that a Russian was first to make a heavier-than-air flight under power was made rather late – in 1949. According to the *Bolshoi Encyclopedia*, Mozhaiski's aircraft was impressively modern, having ailerons, elevators and rudder, a four-wheeled undercarriage with shock-absorbers, a compass, turn-and-bank indicator, and a pair of 30-hp steam engines which he designed himself.

What is known is that Mozhaiski was in 1881 granted a patent for an 'aeronautical device' that was a large monoplane with wings of about 12.2-m (40-ft) span. Its two steam engines were made in England, and were of 10 hp and 20 hp, one driving a tractor propeller at the nose of the machine, the other turning two pusher propellers in slots in the wing structure. According to the *Czarist Military Encyclopedia* of 1914, the test flight was made not in 1882, but 1884, from Krasnoye Selo, near St Petersburg, and the aircraft was flown not by Mozhaiski himself, but by a minion, one I. N. Gulubev. Like du Temple's machine, the Mozhaiski monoplane was launched down an incline and 'flew' about 30 m (100 ft) from the impetus of the launch before falling on one side and smashing a wing. It was progress, perhaps, but scarcely worthy of the Stalinist memory of Mozhaiski as 'the majestic figure standing at the head of the glorious Pleiades of Russian aviation designers and brilliantly characterizing the originality and might of patriotic aviation thought'. The Communists have not lauded another contemporary Russian idea for a steam-powered ornithopter airliner which would have collected passengers from inaccessible areas by means of a powerful electro-magnet on the end of a rope. Presumably intending travellers would have had to have worn magnetic clothing to be sure of a pick-up.

That same year another myopic visionary presented his idea for a steam-powered spaceship – a giant aerial paddle steamer identical to those plying up and down rivers. 'No indication is given as to sustaining power,' a magazine report observed.

'The world's first flight' – yet again

If Mozhaiski is a controversial figure (at least outside the Iron Curtain; within it no-one is permitted to doubt that Mozhaiski really was the first to fly a powered aircraft), so too is the Frenchman Clément Ader. Ader was an electrical engineer from Toulouse who did some work of the development of the telephone before turning to aeronautics. 'Whoever will be master of the sky will be master of the world,' he declared, as if there were insufficient candidates for that title already. Ader's first aircraft was an ornithopter and, like all of its kind, it was a failure. Perhaps influenced by Leonardo da Vinci's advice to 'remember that your flying machine ought not to imitate anything but the bat', Ader's second aircraft, named *Eole*, had folding membraneous wings exactly like those of a bat. A 20-hp steam engine powered the *Eole*, which made a flight of about 50 m (164 ft) at Gretz-Armainvilliers near Paris on 9 October 1890 after taking off from level ground. Two witnesses to the event buried blocks of coal at the spot where *Eole* landed. Forty-seven years later investigators dug up the area to check the Ader claim; they found the coal. Even so, *Eole*'s 'flight' was no more than an uncontrolled hop, and Ader himself admitted 'the necessity for further study'.

The French War Ministry was evidently impressed with Ader's work, and gave him a generous grant for the construction of another machine, which Ader called *Avion*, thus coining the French word for aircraft. *Avion II* was never built, but *Avion III* appeared in 1897, still with those strange bat-wings, but now with two steam engines and propellers and a tricycle undercarriage. The *Avion III*'s boiler stuck up in front of the pilot, who had to peer round it like the driver of a locomotive. On 14 October 1897 Ader stoked up his steam engines at Satory military camp near Versailles; *Avion III* rolled a short way around its circular track,

shot off and ended up in a field. The pro-Ader camp claimed that it actually did fly, then crashed because of a cross-wind. Ader himself later swore that *Eole* had flown 100 m (330 ft) in 1891 and that *Avion III* flew 300 m (985 ft). Both claims were false, indeed could not have been true, for both his bat-planes were uncontrollable and

Great claims were made for the Ader *Avion III* of 1897, but even if it had flown it would have been useless as the aircraft had no means of control. The wings are here seen in the folded position.

unstable. Yet a field at Satory bears this inscription, doubtless taken for gospel truth by successive generations of Frenchmen: 'Here on Satory Field October 14, 1897, Clément Ader succeeded, on the *Avion* which he himself designed and constructed, in taking off from the ground in spite of the rain and the wind and made a controlled flight over 300 metres [984 ft].'

Ader was a fine engineer, but a poor and headstrong designer of aircraft who failed to take heed of the work of other pioneers. His *Avion III* still survives, lurking bat-like in the rafters of the Conservatoire des Arts et Métiers in Paris alongside Louis Blériot's cross-Channel monoplane.

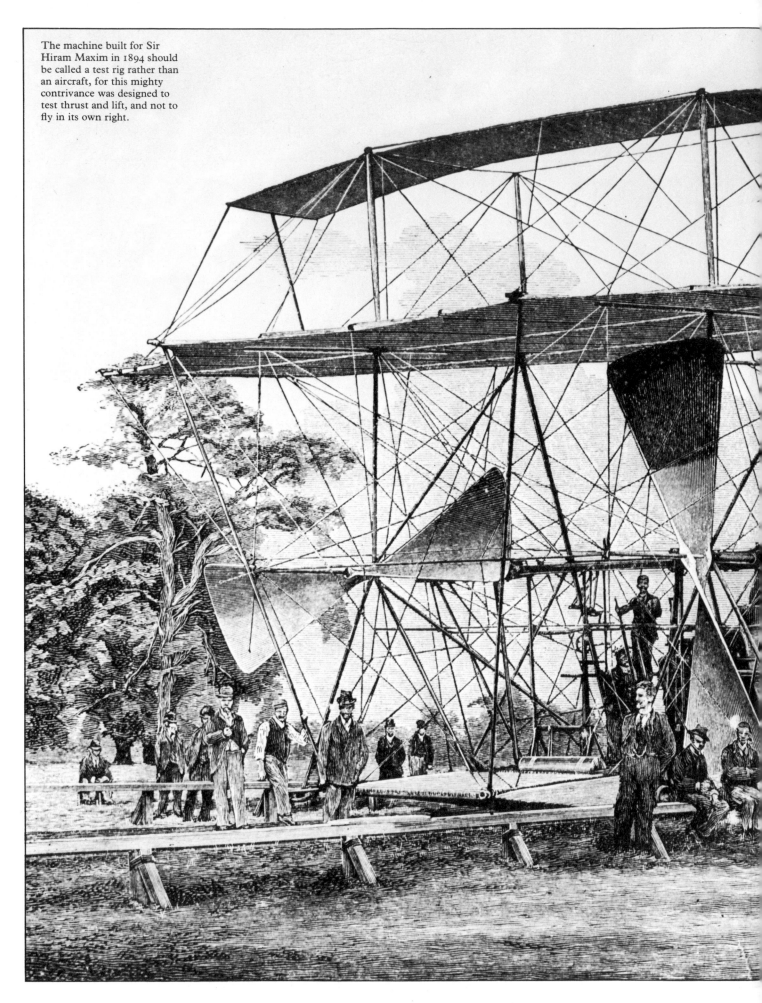

The machine built for Sir Hiram Maxim in 1894 should be called a test rig rather than an aircraft, for this mighty contrivance was designed to test thrust and lift, and not to fly in its own right.

The Maxim test rig

In England, meanwhile, Sir Hiram Stevens Maxim, a naturalized Briton hailing originally from America, was experimenting with an enormous steam-powered biplane. Maxim had made a fortune from the invention of the machine-gun which bore his name and now ploughed it into the pursuit of aeronautics. He foresaw the military potential of flying machines, and like Ader paid little attention to other people's discoveries or to the practical aspects of controlled flight, seeking only to build a machine which would rise from the ground.

In 1889 he started testing various airfoil and propeller designs, whirling them on the end of a rotating arm. He designed and built a lightweight steam engine (proving that at least he understood the most basic need at that time – a powerplant with a good power/weight ratio). In specially rented grounds at Baldwyns Park in Kent he built the machine itself, a mammoth biplane spanning 31.7 m (104 ft) with two 180-hp steam engines to drive its 5.5-m (18-ft) propellers. The thing weighed some 3555 kg (7840 lb), proving that Maxim had not quite achieved that desirable power/weight ratio, and had a crew of four. It was mounted on a length of railway track with an upper restraining rail to prevent the machine rising more than 61 cm (24 in). In June 1892 Maxim was able to report to an American colleague: 'The machine has already been running on the track without the sails [wings] and is all finished except putting on sails. In a few days I shall be conducting experiments as regards the lifting power. I am not using the same steam generator but one in which there is a rapid forced circulation. I think you would like the boiler if you should see it.'

Members of the Aeronautical Society went down to Kent to see Maxim's machine, and very grand they looked, silk-toppered and monocled as they posed self-consciously for a commemorative photograph. Tests proceeded at leisurely pace, climaxing on 31 July 1894 when the biplane ran 180 m (600 ft) down the 550-m (1800-ft) track and rose into the air, carrying three crewmen aloft, but not very far, for as it rose the aircraft fouled the upper guard rail and Maxim was forced to shut off steam. After that he removed the craft's outer wing panels so that never again could it rise, and demonstrated it for charity, in whose name anything still goes.

Maxim's machine was a last grand gesture by the steamers before internal combustion, which had been making great strides in power output and reliability in the latter half of the century, finally provided the key to sustained, controlled flight when the Wright brothers became interested in flight.

Chapter 4

MANY WINGS...

With the lift generated by the double-surfaced cambered wing amply proved by the beginning of the twentieth century, many aeronautical inventors let their imaginations get the better of them: if two sets of wings were good, more sets must be better. The result was a plague of multi-winged aircraft ranging from the impossible 12-winged d'Equevilly machine of 1908 to the eminently sensible Sopwith Triplane of 1916. The triplane configuration was also popular for the heavy weight-lifters of World War I, but reached its nadir with the nine-winged *Capronissimo* behemoth of 1921.

Above: Alliott Verdon Roe in his 1909 machine resorted not only to triplane wings but also a triple tailplane.

Left: A good example of the absurdities perpetrated by some of the early 'designers' is the Marquis d'Equevilly's 1908 multiplane, powered by a tiny 7-hp engine.

When asked what kind of image the term 'old aircraft' calls to mind, the chances are that most people would reply an aircraft with two sets of wings – a biplane. That was how most of the successful early machines looked, not because of the aerodynamic excellence of the configuration, but for reasons of structural expediency. In the earliest years of aviation the materials available did not lend themselves well to the construction of monoplane wings, but by using struts and wires to brace a pair of wings one on top of the other, it was possible to produce a strong, rigid, yet light structure which was free of the flexing problems encountered in monoplanes. Thus biplanes emerged, and such aircraft are still being manufactured today for specialized roles such as competition aerobatics and agricultural aviation.

Sir George Cayley, so often in the forefront of aeronautical pioneering, was first to realize the advantages of multi-winged aircraft. Criticizing Henson's Aerial Steam Carriage (*see Chapter 3*) in an 1843 issue of *The Mechanics' Magazine* he wrote:

'In order to obtain a sufficient quantity of surface to sustain great weights in the air, the extension of the sustaining surface ought not to be made in one plane but in parallel planes one above the other at a convenient distance . . . would it not be more likely to answer the purpose to compact it into the form of a three decker . . .?'

Some experimenters extended Cayley's theory to a seemingly logical conclusion. If three sets of wings were good, then surely four, five, or even more would be better? Such thinking sparked off a brief but splendidly bizarre era of multiplane mania, led by another Englishman named Horatio Frederick Phillips, who conducted some valuable research into the theory of airfoil sections and discovered with the aid of a wind-tunnel that wing sections with greater curvature on their upper surfaces generated lift from the fast-moving low-pressure air across the convex surface. Phillips registered the first of his many airfoil patents in 1884 and in 1893 built a working model aircraft which had 20 wings of 5.8-m (19-ft) span and just 3.8-cm (1½-in) chord. This steam-driven test-rig soon earned the apposite nickname 'Venetian Blind', and was driven around a circular track at Harrow near London in May of that year, reportedly rising 1 m (3 ft) in the air and flying, tethered, at 64 kph (40 mph).

A piloted version followed a year later, the intervening 12 months giving Phillips time to hand-carve its 20 yellow-pine 'wings' or vanes and to engineer its 22-hp water-cooled engine. It was all to no avail, however, for the Phillips Multiplane proved quite uncontrollable. Phillips was undeterred: in 1907 he reappeared with his final masterpiece, which had no fewer than 200 wings set in four frames, which gave it a striking resemblance to a complex bird aviary. During trials at Streatham this craft also is said to have flown and carried Phillips a distance of 152 m (500 ft) through the air. If so, the multiwing king was the first man to fly under power in Britain, and certainly no-one has ever challenged his grand total of 200 wings on one airframe, or seems likely to.

Vain efforts in the New World
But some have tried. An American named Roshon built an aircraft with 24 wings which must have been an instantly forgettable craft, for even a contemporary journal relegated it to a section headed 'cemetery of good ideas', wherein might also have been buried the 12-winged fantasy built by the Marquis d'Equevilly in 1908. This absurdity was held together (or apart, depending one one's point of view) by a pair of metal hoops in the midst of which its pilot stood in a circular cage behind its 7-hp engine.

Californian Professor Zerbe settled for a mere five wings arranged in staggered formation like the steps of a staircase. A photograph of this 1910 multiplane shows it dashing headlong across Dominguez Field near Los Angeles in a great cloud of dust while a gas balloon floats mockingly overhead. Seconds later one of the Zerbe's

Below : Not content with the problems posed by 12 wings, the Marquis d'Equevilly also tried a 50-wing aircraft of similar configuration. The cyclist in the background looks suitably unimpressed with the machine.

front wheels struck a hole in the ground and the flying staircase flipped over and was wrecked.

Not all the early multiplanes were failures. Alliott Verdon Roe – turning to aviation after a varied career in surveying, tree-planting, fishing, post-office management and marine engineering – became intrigued with the flight of albatrosses during a sea voyage. On his return to England young Roe experimented with paper gliders which he launched from a top window of the family home in Manchester, much to the delight of inmates of an adjacent lunatic asylum, one of whom confided to a nurse that there was another of his kind living next door. Spurred by winning £75 in a model aircraft contest held in London in 1907, Roe built a full-size biplane which made some tentative hops from the motor racing circuit at Brooklands in 1908, then moved to an abandoned railway arch on desolate Lea Marshes in Essex, where he built a tiny triplane which weighed less than 91 kg (200 lb) and was covered in brown wrapping paper. He called it the Bull's-Eye Avroplane after the brand-name of men's trouser braces whose manufacturer had supported him, if the pun can be forgiven. In July 1909 the Roe Triplane made the first official powered flights in Britain by an all-British aircraft. Alliott Roe subsequently developed three other triplane designs, one of which he flew (and crashed three times) at the great Boston-Harvard Aviation Meeting of 1910, winning over the American crowds for good-humoured persistence if not for performance.

Success for the military

World War I produced a rash of multiplanes from virtually every aircraft builder on each of the two sides. Two were outstandingly successful – the Sopwith Triplane and the Fokker Dr I. The Sopwith Triplane was designed by Herbert Smith, who was later responsible for the legendary Camel. The prototype made its first flight on 30 May 1916 with test pilot Harry Hawker at the controls, and so delighted was he with the Triplane's handling that he performed a loop within three minutes of taking off. The triplane configuration, as Sir George Cayley predicted, offered several advantages: the narrow chord wings increased manoeuvrability because changes in centre of pressure at different angles of incidence were small, enabling a short fuselage to be used and thus putting the aircraft's main weight in a small area, further aiding manoeuvrability.

The Sopwith Triplane was immediately liked by its pilots when it entered service early in 1917. No other machine could match its rate of climb, and no other fighter could regularly operate at 6100 m (20,000 ft), a height at which the Triplane frequently patrolled. A German pilot summed up the Triplane's appearance on the Western Front: 'The sight of a Sopwith Triplane formation induced pilots to dive out of range.' Cecil Lewis recalled in his classic

Below: Professor Zerbe's quintuplane makes a dash across its airfield just before coming to grief in a pothole, its overall failure highlighted by the balloon floating serenely overhead.

Sagittarius Rising that the Sopwith Triplane

'remains in my memory as the best – for the actual pleasure of flying – that I ever took up. It was so beautifully balanced, so well-mannered, so feather-light on the stick . . . Other machines were faster, stronger, had better climb or vision; but none was so friendly as the Tripe. After it I never wanted to fly anything but a scout again.'

The dominance of the 'Tripe' did not last long. In Germany the brilliant Reinhold Platz designed for Anthony Fokker the great Dr I triplane, immortalized by Baron Manfred von Richthofen who fought and died in one. The Dr I was designed for all-out manoeuvrability. Devoid of bracing wires, with clean lines and light but rugged construction, the Fokker's feather-light pitch response and instability in yaw enabled a skilled pilot to outfly faster aircraft. The Red Baron himself reported that his blood-red *Dreidecker* 'climbed like a monkey and manoeuvred like the devil'. Significantly, von Richthofen retained the dimunitive triplane long after his unit had re-equipped with faster biplanes, while Ernst Udet, second highest-scoring German ace of World War I, considered it 'the ideal fighting airplane' and even attempted to have a replica built for sport flying when the war ended. So delightful is the Dr I's

handling that the 1917 design is enjoying renewed popularity six decades later as a homebuilt replica project, too late for the unfortunate Udet who committed suicide during World War II.

Wartime multiplane activity was not restricted solely to fighters. Given the lamentable power-to-weight ratios of many contemporary engines, designers of bombers seeking to carry heavy loads were forced to use massive wing areas and, just as Cayley had advised in 1843, they turned to multi-wing configurations.

Caproni's giants
Prominent among them was Count Gianni Caproni di Taliedo, one of those geniuses whose inventions seemed always to be a little too far ahead of their times. Caproni designed his first heavy bomber in 1913, ahead of everyone except Igor Sikorsky whose giant four-engined *Ilya Muromets* (*see Chapter 13*) was the world's first 'jumbo' aircraft. Caproni's big biplane bombers had a demoralizing effect on ground troops during the Austro–Italian conflict, more by virtue of their size and threatening appearance than their destructive power, and led to a series of immense triplane bombers during World War I. The first was designed in mid-1915 and was designated Caproni Ca. 40. With three 200-hp Fiat or

Isotta-Fraschini engines, one pushing and the others driving tractor propellers, the 6440-kg (14,200-lb) behemoth was barely able to get out of its own way and had a maximum speed of 125 kph (78 mph). A later development, the Ca. 42, was equipped with more powerful 400-hp American Liberty engines among others. Though still a clumsy monument to high drag, the Ca. 42 could carry a 1450-kg (3200-lb) bomb load over a long range, but the type was difficult to fly, and being slow, was vulnerable to fighter attack despite an arsenal of defensive weapons, which included machine-guns and even a 25.4-mm cannon on some examples. Twenty-three were built, mostly for the Italian Navy, who used them on night bombing raids and in daylight against the Austrians during the final assault at Vittorio Veneto. Six Ca. 42s were supplied to the British Royal Naval Air Service, though they apparently never left Italy. Inadequate in many ways, Count Caproni's three-winged monsters never the less gave true strategic bombing capability and were to have been mass-produced in the United States until the Armistice halted the project. An airliner version was built after the war: this could carry 17 passengers in a plushly furnished cabin and a further six less comfortably out in the slipstream, but the post-war uncertainty of civil aviation

halted development.

Over in France the great pioneer aviator Gabriel Voisin also built enormous triplane bombers for the French war effort. His aircraft were even bigger than Caproni's, spanning 36 m (118 ft) with four 200-hp engines mounted in tandem pairs. Not only did they have three wings, but also two fuselages, the upper one affording an air gunner a near 360-degree field of fire. Voisin's 1915 design had Salmson radial engines; the 1916 version switched to Hispano Suizas and flew just 35 days after the French high command placed their order for an aircraft capable of carrying a dozen 220-mm ($8\frac{2}{3}$-in) shells. The aircraft never saw service, as Voisin recalled bitterly in his memoirs:

'In 1914, when Chalais-Meudon [a French test centre] was in the hands of men like Martinot Lagarde, Destouches, and Camerman, the construction of this machine would have started simultaneously with the instruction of mechanics and pilots. But the worm which was to eat into French aviation was already in the fruit. The triplane waited uselessly and then, during dismantling, it was destroyed. If this machine had been brought out in the ordinary manner by January 1917 we would have had the means which could not have been foreseen by the enemy, to cut his lines of communication in a few hours and probably to gain six months in the

Below: What could be achieved by the triplane configuration was confirmed by the Fokker Dr I, which was produced in response to the successful Sopwith Triplane, and was unexcelled in manoeuvrability right up to the end of World War I. The face motif on the front of this Dr I shows that this was the personal aircraft of *Leutnant* Werner Voss, fourth on the list of German aces with 48 'kills'. Voss was himself shot down and killed on 23 September 1917 in a Dr I after an epic single-handed dogfight with a number of British aces.

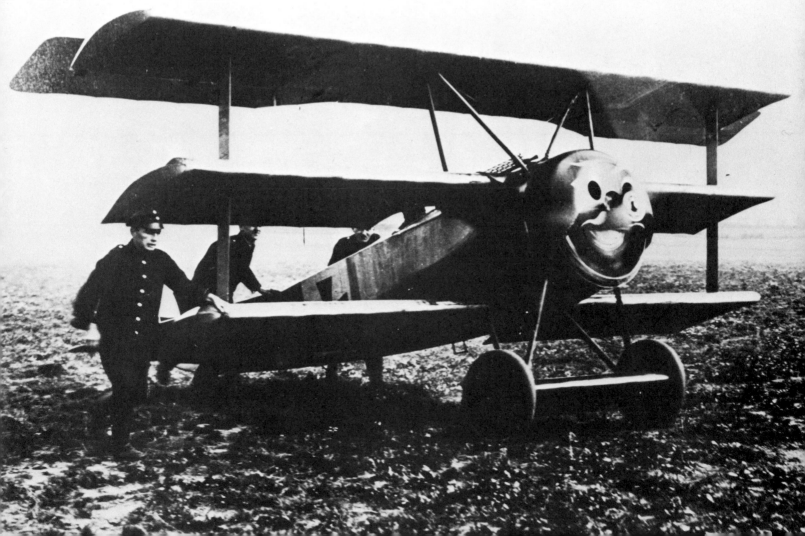

conduct of the war. I had realised for some time that French aviation was doomed. This fate gradually became a certainty and I planned with fortitude for the reconversion of our factories.'

The embittered Voisin never got over his disappointment and gave up aviation altogether and took to building automobiles.

Eccentricity runs riot

Another eccentric planemaker set about building a massive multiplane about this time. Noel Pemberton-Billing, a wealthy yacht-broker, gun-runner and aircraft manufacturer (he established the Supermarine company, makers of the Schneider Trophy racers and Battle of Britain Spitfire), described as 'tall, slick, monocled and iron-jawed' by contemporary society columnists, learned to fly in 24 hours to win a £500 wager with Frederick Handley Page and subsequently served with the Royal Naval Air Service, from which his 'tempestuous temperament' earned him an early retirement, though not before he had helped to organize the first aerial attack on the Zeppelin sheds on Lake Constance. In 1916

the irrepressible Pemberton-Billing was standing for Parliamentary election in an East End borough of London, promising the Zeppelin-fearing electorate that he had a machine 'which carries armament before which a Zeppelin would turn back and never come here again'. London, he promised the voters, would be so well guarded that in the unlikely event that any of mad Count von Zeppelin's marauding sky-monsters managed to escape, they would certainly never dare to return. Pemberton-Billing's pitch was indeed impressive, but also ill-founded, for the Zeppelin-busting Supermarine P.B.9 crashed a few days after its first flight.

Pemberton-Billing took that blow squarely on his iron jaw and bounced back with a second airship killer – the Supermarine Nighthawk. This aircraft had four sets of wings and carried three gunners – one facing to the rear, one up front, and another in a forward upper turret wielding a $1\frac{1}{2}$-pounder Davis gun capable of swatting the German gasbags out of the sky. A searchlight was mounted in the Nighthawk's

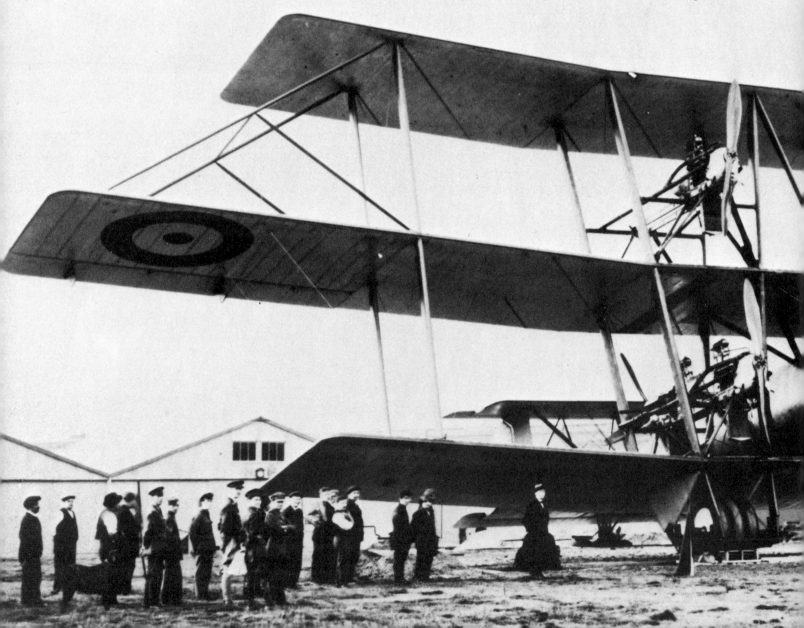

nose to help the gunners aim at night (as its name implies, the Nighthawk was designed as a night-fighter), and the aircraft reputedly carried 1016 kg (2240 lb) of fuel for its two 100-hp Anzani engines – enough for it to remain in the air for up to 18 hours while loitering at speeds as slow as 56 kph (35 mph). Pemberton-Billing promised that he would fly over the East End to drop a vote of thanks to the people when they elected him. The East-Enders saved him the trouble by choosing someone else for their Member of Parliament.

The Zeppelin raids on England had done little damage to property or life, but they mortally offended British pride. The call went out for retribution, to give the 'Hun' a taste of his own medicine by bombing Berlin. The problem was that there were no British aircraft available which could even fly to the German capital and back, much less carry bombs there. One patriot who felt he could fill this gap and strike a blow at the Kaiser was a Surrey building contractor, W. G. Tarrant, whose company had been involved in wartime contract work

manufacturing wooden aircraft components. Tarrant hired Walter Henry Barling to design the aircraft, which was to be a 'bloody paralyzer' of a triplane made entirely of home-grown timber and constructed using a largely female work force, according to the terms of the contract issued by the Ministry of Munitions.

When it appeared, too late for its intended purpose, the Tarrant Tabor was the largest aircraft built in Britain, bigger even than a World War II Lancaster or Flying Fortress. It spanned 40 m (131 ft 3 in) from tip to tip of its middle wing, and had a cavernous 22.25-m (73-ft) fuselage of monocoque construction formed from ply skinning over Warren-girder type circular formers. Six 450-hp Napier Lion engines powered the mammoth: two pairs in push-pull tandem between lower and middle wings, and another two tractor engines between middle and top planes. The Tabor stood as high as a four-storey house, and its height, and particularly the location of its upper engines, brought about its speedy demise.

On 26 May 1919 the giant Tabor was

An effort to get the maximum amount of aircraft into the minimum amount of space resulted in the ill-fated Tarrant Tabor. This monster of the air (or of the ground, as events were to prove) was powered by six 500-hp Napier Lion engines, the location of the top pair proving the main reasons for the Tabor's crash.

winched out of the balloon shed at the Royal Aircraft Establishment at Farnborough along a specially built railway track. Some 508 kg (1120 lb) of lead was loaded into the nose at the last moment when some final calculations showed that the aircraft might be tail heavy, and the long, wearisome process of hand-starting the six Napier Lions began. With all engines running the pilot, Captain F. G. Dunn, and his co-pilot, Captain P. T. Rawlings, began taxi trials. Also aboard were a technical observer from Tarrant's, a fitter, an engineer officer, and two foremen from the RAE, one of whom takes up the story:

'He [Dunn] now opened up all the bottom engines full out, and I noticed the tail climbing higher; Dunn never looked astern, at the engines or aside. Rawlings was still sitting sideways on his legs. Realising we were about to attempt flight, I settled back down the ladder and hooked one foot around a bomb-rack girder. The Tabor was bumping and bouncing very badly, and I looked back along the fuselage at the tail and was alarmed at its height. After this I heard the roar of the top engines and looked at their revs – they were already at 1800, a very sudden increase. Then on looking at the landing gear I saw the wheels were well clear of the long grass . . . I next saw a shower of earth thrown from the landing gear on the starboard side. Very shortly after this I actually saw Dunn and Rawlings thrown from the aircraft when it hit.'

What happened was that Dunn had opened up the top engines, which had previously been throttled back, and the sudden extra thrust so far above the aircraft's centreline caused it to nose-over and bury its forward fuselage in the earth just as it was about to leave the ground. The two pilots died shortly afterwards of their injuries and Tarrant, perhaps fortunately for other aviators, never again dabbled with aviation.

Larger and yet larger

Designer Walter Barling did, though. He went to America, where the zealous airpower fanatic General 'Billy' Mitchell provided him with a $375,000 contract to build a bomber capable of carrying a 2268-kg (5000-lb) bombload for 12 hours at 160 kph (100 mph). Not surprisingly the Barling NBL-1 bore a strong resemblance to the Tarrant Tabor, though its triplane wings spanned 3.35 m (11 ft) less and its six 12-cylinder Liberty engines were all mounted on the same level, between the lower and middle wings. It was an aircraft 'more likely to antagonize the air than to pass through it' one unkind observer remarked, but pass through the air it did, on 22 August 1923 from Wilbur Wright Field at Dayton, Ohio, whence it had been railroaded from the Witteman-Lewis Aircraft Company's works in New Jersey. Barling was aboard for that 20-minute maiden flight and later that year the Barling bomber flew to the International Air Race at St Louis with Major General Mason Patrick, chief of the Army Air Service, as a passenger. It later carried a 2000-kg (4408-lb) load up to 2,050 m (6722 ft). But with Billy Mitchell's proposed bomb load the burly Barling could not top 160 kph (100 mph) and had a range of 275 km (170 miles) rather than the 1930 km (1200 miles) the general wanted. It flew around (slowly) for years, appearing as a curiosity at airshows, and was eventually broken up in 1928, save for its ten huge undercarriage wheels which are preserved at Wright-Patterson Air Force base from where the triplane made its first flight.

Perhaps the most wondrous of all the multiplanes was Count Caproni's final fling – a nine-winged, 100-passenger flying houseboat which looked exactly like a flying galleon or, as events turned out, a non-flying galleon. Caproni's Ca. 60, unofficially named *Capronissimo* and *Noviplano*, had three sets of triplane wings arranged in tandem on top of an immense hull. Eight 400-hp Liberty engines, four pushing, four pulling, were supposed to make the thing fly, and provision was made for engineers to walk along the extended nacelles to attend the motors in flight, a

wise precaution Liberty engines being what they were.

This preposterous craft was launched on Lake Maggiore on 21 January 1921 in the presence of the American Ambassador to Italy, his country having done the dubious favour of supplying its engines. The first trial hop in March confirmed what many observers had already opined – that the *Noviplano* was woefully unstable longitudinally. Test pilot Semprini, snapped by a photographer just before the first flight proper, had the look of a man with something on his mind, but he was persuaded to fly the weird triple triplane, and with sandbags representing a load of 60 passengers he gave the 3200 Liberty 'horses' their head and managed to coax *Capronissimo* aloft to all of 20 m (66 ft) before its nose dipped and the aerial sailing ship dived into the lake and broke up. Semprini was fished out and the wreck was salvaged for rebuilding. A fire conveniently destroyed its remains before the work was completed, whereupon Count Caproni decided that enough was enough. No nine-winged phoenix ever did arise from *Capronissimo*'s ashes, much to the relief of Signor Semprini, one imagines. Plans for an even bigger, 150-passenger version were dropped, and the era of the amazing multiplanes ended not with a bang but a splash.

Below : The Caproni Ca.60 must surely be one of aviation's most emphatic failures. The *Capronissimo* justly deserves a number of accolades, but success in the air cannot be one of them, for this monstrous creation crashed on its first and only flight in March 1921, showing clearly that the design of giant aircraft was still a difficult process.

Chapter 5

...BUT NO TAILS

The concept of the flying wing is one of those notions which is eminently attractive in theory, but immensely difficult to realize in practice. The argument in favour of flying wings is irrefutable: do away with all those parts of the aircraft which do not provide lift but do generate masses of drag, and you will be left with a highly efficient craft capable of higher performance and greater range than its conventional counterpart. But the efforts of great designers such as Alexander Lippisch showed the scope of the practical problem, and when John Northrop had apparently solved this problem, entrenched interests killed the type . . . or have they?

Above : The aerodynamic benefits of a tailless layout can be seen in the Armstrong Whitworth AW.52G test glider.

Left : The compactness of tailless designs is clearly seen on the somewhat ungainly Waterman 'Whatsit' experimental lightplane.

WHILE MULTIPLANE ENTHUSIASTS were busily piling up wings, a young British Army lieutenant, invalided home from the Boer War, was experimenting with ways to produce a practical, stable flying machine by reducing the number of surfaces and dispensing with tail units, horizontal stabilizers and rudders altogether.

John William Dunne became interested in aviation as a child. After reading Jules Verne's *Clipper of the Clouds* he had a vivid dream in which he sailed through the air in a vessel which required no steering. The notion nagged away at him until 1901, when convalescence from a bout of enteric fever gave him the opportunity to address the problems of flight and to search for an aircraft configuration with inherent stability.

Dunne found inspiration in the winged seed of the Javanese Zanonia plant, whose kidney-shaped leaves glide gently to the ground. He built models with V-shaped wings like arrowheads which flew admirably, with extraordinary stability. Encouraged by his author friend H. G. Wells (who used him as the basis for his character **Captain Douglas** in the novel *Bealby*) Dunne sought out a partner with practical aeronautical experience to assist him in full-size experiments and teamed up with Colonel John Capper, Superintendent of His Majesty's Balloon Factory at South Farnborough in Hampshire.

Their first aircraft, the Dunne D.1, was ready in the spring of 1907. It was a single-seat glider with arrow-shaped biplane wings. Great secrecy surrounded their work, and Farnborough was deemed far too public for test flying. Dunne, Capper and an entourage of army engineers travelled north to a lonely spot at Glen Tilt, on the Marquis of Tullibardine's Scottish estate at Blair Atholl, in Perthshire, where they set up camp. Capper made the first brief flight and assured his masters at the War Office:

'The result, though to an unskilled eye merely disastrous, in effect showed that Lieutenant Dunne's calculations were entirely correct; the machine remaining poised during a period of eight seconds. The weight of the operator was not however placed quite right and instead of gliding away downhill it settled down, breaking one arm on a stone wall.'

The aircraft's broken 'arm' was soon repaired and two Buchet engines totalling 15 hp were fitted. By now rumours of strange goings on at Glen Tilt had attracted newspaper reporters and even German spies to investigate 'the mystery on the moor'. Dunne painted the aircraft in stripes for camouflage. Whether it fooled the snoopers is doubtful; it certainly made no difference to the D.1, which stubbornly refused to fly before the bitter cold of a Scottish winter began to snap at the experimenters' hands, and the team headed back south.

By the following summer the aircraft had been rebuilt with a 25-hp R.E.P. engine. On Dunne's own admission this D.4 was more of a hopper than a flier. It did make eight flights late in 1908, but the longest was barely 36 m (120 ft) and the War Office declined further financial support for his experiments.

Success comes to Dunne

It was a turning point for Dunne. Lord Tullibardine immediately offered to help, and with Capper and his assistant, Captain Carden, they set up the Blair Atholl Aeroplane Syndicate and had Short Brothers build them a new tailless biplane with a 60-hp Green engine driving two propellers.

The D.5 was a two-seater which Dunne elected to test fly himself. Mindful of his weak heart (and perhaps of the cost of the machine) the Syndicate insisted that he confine himself to tests 'and not try for a pilot's certificate or anything of that sort' and away he went. 'It was a rather exciting episode,' Dunne recalled later. 'The thing got off too soon, bounced, and when I recovered my scattered wits I found it

Jules Verne's novel *Clipper of the Clouds* may have proved an inspiration to many, but the aerial dreadnought of the novel, with its multitude of lifting rotors, is manifestly impossible even by today's standards.

roaring away over the aerodrome boundary, climbing evenly, and steady as a rock. So I left well alone, and allowed it to look after itself. This it did till the engine gave out (usually a matter of minutes in those days.)'

This recalcitrant motor put Dunne and his D.5 into the marsh at the end of Eastchurch aerodrome, in Essex, where the team had moved after leaving Scotland. It was the first of many such soggy arrivals, but during the spring of 1910 his weird arrow-shaped aircraft became a familiar sight in the area and was noted for the steadiness with which it flew. The tests culminated in a triumphant 1.25-km (2-mile) flight during which Dunne never touched the controls (his boyhood dream come true!), and a demonstration in front of Orville Wright, during which Dunne was able to make notes on the aircraft's performance whilst airborne to emphasize its hands-off stability, and landed with both arms raised in the air. His pencil scratchings on a flimsy piece of paper were the first airborne notes of an experimental test pilot.

So delighted was he that Dunne concluded 'one may eat, drink, smoke, click a camera, take off one's coat or do a hundred other things' in one of his aircraft. The D.5 had combined elevators and ailerons (what are now called elevons) at the tips of its wings. These were operated by two levers which could be locked into position on a ratchet to maintain a desired attitude, and the machine's stability vindicated Dunne's theories about the tailless configuration.

The trouble was that while they did indeed vindicate the theory, they did so only up to a point. So confident was Dunne that he built a monoplane, the D.7, which was displayed at the 1911 Olympia Aero Show in London, and began making deliberate attempts to upset the machine's equilibrium in flight by letting go of the controls during steep, low-level turns. Even the most forgiving aircraft will bite when sorely tried, and sure enough Dunne suffered four major crashes for his foolhardiness.

Dunne's final designs were built during 1911–1912. Reverting to the biplane configuration he rebuilt the D.5 with a 50-hp Gnome rotary engine and dual controls. Captain Carden, who had but one hand, used this machine to gain his Royal Aero Club Aviator's Certificate in June 1912. In 1913 the aircraft was flown to France for tests by the French Aeronautic Corps, during which Commandant Felix of the Nieuport company astonished crowds at a Deauville flying meeting by stepping from the cockpit and walking along the aircraft's lower wing in flight.

Three Dunne tailless biplanes were built by the Burgess Company of Marblehead,

Massachusetts in 1916 and evaluated by the US Army, but by then the ailing Dunne had broken down from overwork and been advised by his doctors to give up aviation, which he did, devoting his time to writing a book about the nature of the universe and the relationships of dreams to future events (*An Experiment With Time*) which was to make him more famous than his 'auto-safety' self-balancing flying wings. The Dunne biplane configuration has been resurrected lately in several successful hang-glider designs, while the 1930s saw a revival of British tailless aircraft experiments with the Westland Pterodactyls.

Tailless Pterodactyls

The Pterodactyls were the brainchild of Professor Geoffrey Hill, whose brother Roderick commanded experimental flying at Farnborough, Dunne's old stamping ground, in the years following World War I. Like Dunne, Hill started with gliders before gaining the co-operation of the Westland Aircraft Company in launching a series of powered flying 'reptiles' which began with a 32-hp single-seater (now preserved at the Science Museum in London) which first flew in December 1925. Hill and Westland had plans for a whole series of the Pterrible Pterodactyls, including a flying-boat and an airliner, but only four were built, the last being the most bizarre Pterodactyl Mark V which had a 600-hp Rolls-Royce Goshawk steam-cooled engine and was intended as a fighter. The theory was that the tailless configuration would give the rear gunner an almost unlimited field of fire with his pair of synchronized Vickers guns.

Test pilot Harald Penrose's first experience in the beast was not unlike Dunne's.

'The first take-off was trickier than anything I had ever imagined. The machine lurched and bucketed over the ground, and swayed and yawed so disconcertingly that I thought I would have to abandon the attempt – but a ground discontinuity suddenly threw the machine up and once airborne it began to build up a pitching oscillation because I overcontrolled through inexperience with its longitudinal sensitivity. Nevertheless, once high enough to breath freely, I felt I had command, and presently exploration of each control in turn showed that normal flight was reasonably conventional, except that laterally the machine was a big one, and longitudinally it was very small.'

Penrose was soon demonstrating the Pterodactyl's stability, and even performing aerobatics as well as flying it inverted. But a landing accident damaged the sole Mark V and further work on Hill's designs – described as products of the 'chip, clip, chop, crop and lop' school of design – was

abandoned in the mid-1930s, just when
tailless experimentation in Nazi Germany
was beginning to yield results for the work
of the Horten brothers and Doctor Alexander Lippisch.

Reimar and Walter Horten trod the
classic path of aeronautical discovery, starting out with models, then progressing to
gliders and eventually to powered aircraft.
Their first tailless design, the Ho I sailplane,
won a prize at the 1934 Rhön soaring competitions, but the brothers were not satisfied
with its performance and burned it.

There followed a series of ever more
radical sailplane designs, including one
with a parabolic wing shaped like a crescent
moon, before they moved on to a two-seat
twin-engined flying wing which made extensive use of the then revolutionary concept of bonded plastic construction; a 60-
passenger military transport powered by
six 600-hp BMW engines which was under
construction at Göttingen when the war
ended (Reimar Horten later reworked this
Ho VIII as a tailless cargo plane for Argentina's Instituto Technico); and the final,
most advanced design of them all – the Ho
IX twin-jet flying wing fighter which was
the Hortens' first design specifically intended as a combat aircraft. Known as the
Gotha 229, the fighter first flew in 1944, but
the second prototype (the only one com-

pleted with jet engines) was destroyed in a
forced landing early in its test programme.
A third airframe was captured incomplete
at the Gotha works at Friedrichshode by
American troops in April 1945. The unique
jet was shipped to England where some
thought was given to completing it and
installing British powerplants, but government officials baulked at the idea and the
Go 229 v3 was taken to the United States,
where it remains in store for the National
Air & Space Museum.

The 'Devil's Sled'

The US Army was also first to meet with
the fruits of Alexander Lippisch's labours,
though in less peaceful circumstances, for
they came hurtling down on to the serried
ranks of US 8th Air Force's Flying For-
tresses and Liberators bombing Germany.

The new fighter was the Messerschmitt
Me 163 *Komet,* otherwise known as the
Devil's Sled, the most extraordinary combat aircraft to see service in World War II
and one which was frequently as lethal to its
own pilots as it was to the aircraft of the
enemy.

The *Komet* was the product of more than
two decades of patient and persistent
research and experimentation. Alexander
Lippisch designed his first tailless glider in
1921. Ten years later he had progressed to a

triangular wing form which he called 'delta', and his Delta I was ready for demonstration to top German aviation ministry officials at Berlin's Templehof airport. The bureaucrats were sceptical. After all, Lippisch's aircraft looked like nothing they had ever seen before, and even though test pilot Günther Grönhoff performed a low-level aerobatic routine (even spinning the 30-hp Bristol Cherub-powered delta), they remained unconvinced. Lippisch would not get an airworthiness certificate, they declared, until he put tails on his aircraft.

Though the pundits wrote him off as a crank, Lippisch refused to give in. An order came in for a new machine, Delta III, which was to be built by Focke-Wulf in Bremen, and the great pre-war German airshow flier Gerhard Fieseler also enlisted Lippisch's help in designing a two-seat tailless touring aircraft for the 1932 *Europarundflug* – the air races and trials then held every four years. Fieseler's F3 *Wespe* (Wasp) or Delta IVb had delta wings which folded (*Rundflug* aircraft had to be able to fit into a small storage shed) and two engines arranged in a centreline-thrust push-pull configuration. Fieseler flew it before Lippisch was fully satisfied with the design. He crashed, and rapidly lost interest in tailless aircraft. Lippisch meanwhile had completed Delta III, which also had tractor and pusher engines, and immediately set about rebuilding the *Wespe*. His test pilot Grönhoff had been killed in a gliding accident, and lacking a more experienced flier he hired a young man named Wiegmeier, who proceeded to crash both Deltas III and IV on consecutive flights. This recklessness brought Wiegmeier's test flying career to a speedy end: Lippisch fired him.

The crashes attracted attention from the *Reichsluftfahrtministerium* (RLM, the State Ministry of Aviation), who ordered an investigation into Lippisch's designs. The crash commission duly concluded that tailless aircraft 'had neither practical value nor development potential' and forbade further work on them. Luckily for Lippisch the director of the *Deutsches Forschungsinstitut für Segelflug* (German Research Institute for Gliding) had enough 'pull' within the RLM to have the decision reversed, and Lippisch was able to rebuild the *Wespe* once again as the DFS 39 Delta IVc, a single-engined two-seater with a drastically modified wing planform incorporating sharply drooped tips. The modified type was awarded a certificate of airworthiness in 1936 and won Lippisch leadership of the design team for *Projekt X*.

Projekt X was accorded the highest grade of secrecy, so much so that those connected with it claimed documents should have been labelled DESTROY BEFORE READING. The heart of *Projekt X* was a rocket engine developed by Hellmuth Walter. Lippisch's task was to design a tailless aircraft to go with it, and his labour was made none the easier by the fanatical secrecy. Even he was not allowed to have blueprints of the powerplant for the airframe he was designing.

A practical aircraft?

The result of this clandestine effort was a tailless rocket research craft designated the DFS 194 which began flight trials with a 400-kg (882-lb) thrust liquid-fuel Walter rocket motor at the Baltic coast test site of Peenemünde in August 1940. While test pilot Heini Dittmar flew this test bed, reaching 550 kph (341.8 mph) in level flight, Lippisch and his team pressed on with the next stage of *Projekt X* at the Messerschmitt *Werke* in Augsburg. The ultimate aim was to produce a rocket-powered interceptor fighter. Three development prototypes were ordered by the RLM and the first two were completed by the spring of 1941, when unpowered gliding flights began from the factory airfield. Incredibly the engineless Messerschmitt Me 163 attained a top speed of 850 kph (528 mph) in a dive test. 'What kind of engine is installed?' was the question posed by *Generalluftzeugmeister* (Chief of Air Equipment) Ernst Udet to Lippisch as the aircraft flashed past him at over 645 kph (400 mph). One can imagine the look on Udet's face when *Herr Doktor* Lippisch replied casually 'None'.

Dittmar's demonstration convinced Udet that *Projekt X* deserved high priority and within weeks the first powered flights were made. On 2 October 1941 Heini Dittmar cast off from a Messerschmitt Bf 110 towplane at 4000 m (13,125 ft), fired the Me 163V-1's rocket motor and accelerated rapidly past that magic figure of 1000 kph (622 mph) for the first time in history. Udet was ecstatic. 'Fit guns!' he urged Lippisch.

Below: The Messerschmitt Me 163B was aerodynamically successful, its failings resulting from the need to rely on a liquid-propellant rocket motor for propulsion. This Walter motor burned fuel at a voracious rate, but any shock to the small quantities of fuel left in the tanks after a flight could lead to detonation and inevitable destruction of aircraft and pilot.

Above : The huge Northrop XB-35 flying wing bomber, which first flew in June 1946, brought a new dimension to the concept of heavy bombing. The aerodynamic cleanliness of the aircraft had important performance benefits, while the elimination of non-contributory portions such as the fuselage and tailplane allowed a higher proportion of the total weight to consist of payload. In the event, however, the manufacturers of more conventional aircraft capitalized on the conservatism of US air force commanders to ensure that the XB-35 did not advance beyond the prototype stage.

But the designer knew that his *Komet* was still far from being a viable weapon, and Udet's dream of a rocket interceptor decimating the Allied bombers had yet to reach fruition.

When it did, the dream proved more of a nightmare, for the production Me 163B's 1500-kg (3307-lb) thrust Walter HWK 109–509 rocket motor was fuelled with a highly volatile mixture of *C-stoff* (methyl alcohol, hydrazine hydrate and water) and *T-stoff* (hydrogen peroxide with additional hydrocarbon stabilizers) which would explode at the least provocation. By way of caution to new *Komet* pilots, technicians would allow the merest drop of one to fall onto the other. 'The results were instantaneous,' wrote Mano Ziegler in his book *Rocket Fighter*, 'a hiss, a bang, and a jet of flame all in one'. Hardly reassuring, for a *Komet* pilot sat in the middle of more than 2000 kg (4409 lb) of this witches' brew, the brief and violent union of which thrust his tiny aircraft in a zoom climb to 12,000 m (39,370 ft) in 3 minutes 30 seconds.

The *Luftwaffe*'s plan was that *Komets*, perhaps thousands of them, would be launched as soon as the formations of enemy bombers were sighted. After rocketing high above them, the *Komet* pilots would use their remaining fuel to dive at high speed through the ranks of bombers firing on them with the Me 163B's two 20-mm MG 151/20 or 30-mm MK 108 cannon, or with the SG 500 *Jagdfaust* (hunter's fist) 50-mm (1.97-in) weapon system, which fired shells vertically upwards from the top surface of the *Komet*'s wing when a bomber's shadow triggered its photo-electric cell

firing circuit. Although pilots of *Jagdgesch-wader* 400 who flew the rocket fighter in combat did manage to destroy American raiders, the *Komet* proved more vulnerable than its targets. The Walter rocket motor consumed fuel at almost twice the expected rate, leaving pilots with high-performance gliders which were easy prey for USAAF North American P-51 Mustangs. And even when they returned safely to base the *Komet* crews were far from safe, for the remaining dregs of *C-stoff* and *T-stoff* were liable to explode and destroy man and machine in one bright, vicious flash if the skid landing was less than feathery-soft. Planned developments of the *Komet* were in hand when the war ended, but Alexander Lippisch had already grown tired of both Messerschmitt and the *Luftwaffe* and retired to a research institute in Vienna where he designed a delta-wing supersonic interceptor which later inspired Convair's XF-92A delta wing research craft and F-102 Delta Dagger fighter.

The Northrop wings

John Knudsen Northrop was a contemporary of Lippisch, and like the German became fascinated by tailless 'all-wing' aircraft which would reduce parasite drag (drag created by every protruding component of an aircraft which does not directly contribute to lift) and thus give greater fuel efficiency, longer range and heavier payloads. Northrop built his first 'all-wing' aircraft in 1928, though he retained conventional tail surfaces. His (and the world's) first true all-wing flew in 1940 from a site in California's Mojave Desert. It was designated N-1M and consisted of nothing but an 11.6-m (38-ft) wing with a pair of buried 65-hp Lycoming engines (driving pusher propellers) and a tiny pimple of a cockpit canopy. Northrop was fanatical about ridding his wings of every unnecessary protuberance. 'What you don't put into an airplane can't give no trouble' was one of his maxims, and his ultimate aim was for an aircraft which had a wing and nothing else – no protruding cockpit, engines or tail fins, nothing to spoil the efficiency of the clean lifting surface.

Just like Dunne and Penrose, test pilot Vance Breese found himself airborne unexpectedly when a hillock threw the N-1M into the air during fast taxi trials. Breese kept the aircraft close to the ground 'to make the crash a bit easier'. But there was no crash. Although a *Time* magazine man described the N-1M as 'a ruptured, weather-racked duck, too fatigued to tuck in its wings', the little yellow aircraft flew extremely well. General 'Hap' Arnold saw it and encouraged Northrop to design an all-wing heavy bomber. Four one-third scale flying 'models' were built while Northrop proceeded with parallel development of other tailless projects: the XP-56 'pursuit ship' fighter built entirely of magnesium, which might well have been the fastest of all piston-engined aircraft had development not been halted in 1944; the MX-324 tailless glider which was flown with rocket power in July 1944 when rumours were rife about a secret German tailless rocket fighter (the Me 163); and the

XP-79 Flying Ram which was jet-powered and designed to down enemy aircraft by deliberate ramming, which it was supposed to be able to do ten times per mission without sustaining serious damage. No-one ever got the chance to find out, for the XP-79, which was surely the only aircraft specifically designed for midair collisions, rammed the earth during its maiden flight on 12 September 1945, killing test pilot Harry Crosby and completely destroying itself. At the war's end aerial ramming became an anti-social activity and the lethal flying wing was forgotten.

Meanwhile the one-third scale N-9M test programme had led to Jack Northrop's largest, most incredible flying wings of all. Faced with the distinct possibility of a British defeat in the war in Europe, America's most pressing need in 1941 was for a bomber with intercontinental range which could strike Germany and return home. On paper Northrop's flying wings looked like the answer. They could fly perhaps 40 per cent farther than conventional aircraft at greater speeds and on less power, so the US Army gave the go-ahead for an aircraft of breathtaking size which spanned 52.4 m (172 ft), had a gross weight of 78,845 kg (165,000 lb) and could carry a 23,225-kg (51,200-lb) bombload. Four 3000-hp Pratt & Whitney Wasp Major engines driving contra-rotating pusher propellers powered this behemoth, which had a crew of 15 and was to have been defended by 20 remotely-controlled 12.7-mm (0.5-in) machine-guns.

Below: After examination of the aerodynamic problems of tailless aircraft with their AW.52G glider, Armstrong Whitworth moved on to the AW.52 twin-jet experimental aircraft of 1947. Although great benefits were possible with such aircraft, financial problems finally curtailed the programme in 1950, much to the loss of the company and the country.

Construction of the prototype XB-35 took the entire duration of the war, with a firm of elevator manufacturers being called in to give advice on the design of its wing structure! The first of 15 aircraft ordered flew on 25 June 1946, and it was a sensation. Nothing had ever been seen like the awesome flying wing, which still looks futuristic three decades on. The XB-35 was worthy of the creations of Lieutenant Dunne's great friend H. G. Wells but, as so often with radical ideas, it was the mundane which caused its failure. The XB-35's massive propellers gave nothing but trouble: gears stripped, blade pitch reversed in flight, propellers 'ran away', uncontrollable fires started. The only possible solution was the use of jet engines, and Northrop's jet-powered YB-49 flew in October 1947. With eight 1814-kg (4000-lb) thrust Allison J35 engines it was the most powerful aircraft at that time built, and it climbed faster and flew farther than any other bomber. Confidence ran high, and the USAF ordered 30 YRB-49s for the long range reconnaissance role. Even the fatal inflight breakup of the second prototype failed to dampen spirits.

Then came a bitter blow: the USAF contract was abruptly terminated, allegedly because of top-ranking feeling that the flying wing was just too good to be true, and the money diverted to the purchase of the much-vaunted Convair B-36 *(see Chapter 13)*. The YB-49 made a flag-waving trip from Edwards Air Force Base in California (named after the dead pilot of the crashed aircraft) to Washington, D.C. at 823 kph (511.2 mph), 160 kph (100 mph) faster than the favoured B-36, but it was too late. Both good and true, the YB-49 and the all-wing concept was dead in America, and was soon to die in Britain, where the Armstrong Whitworth company experimented briefly with two jet-powered AW.52 flying wings between 1947 and 1950.

The ultimate expression of the flying-wing concept is perhaps to be found in the Northrop YB-49 jet bomber project. Yet again, though, the promise of the type seemed to be too good to be true, and it was cancelled, despite the clear advantages of the flying wing in terms of low drag and low structure weight.

Chapter 6
DUCKS

Like the flying wing, the tail-first (or canard) aircraft offers many advantages if the adventurous designer can evade the many problems associated with such a configuration. It is in the military field that the canard has occasionally come into its own, but there seems every reason to believe that in the present fuel-starved times the lightplane canards pioneered by Burt Rutan in the United States may offer a new lease of life to such aircraft – if the major builders will allow it.

Above : The Rutan Vari-Eze is another variant on the canard theme, in this instance tailored to high performance.

Left : One of the fascinating designs originating from the drawing board of the prolific designer Burt Rutan, the Vari-Viggen is a compact canard lightplane of good performance.

T AIL-FIRST AIRCRAFT are called canards: *canard* is French for duck, and aircraft with their wings set at the rear and their tails up towards the nose are supposed to look like ducks in flight. But *canard* is one of those subtle *doubles entendres*: it also means a hoax, a joke, an absurdity, and when one looks at some canard aircraft it is no easy task to decide just which was meant.

Today, and indeed for most of aviation's history, the tail-first configuration has been considered highly unorthodox, yet paradoxically the world's first successful powered flying machine, and the first aircraft to fly in Europe, were both canards.

To understand why anyone should want to put an aircraft's tail (the very word suggests it should be at the back) on its nose, except perhaps out of some personal caprice, it is necessary to consider a little aerodynamic theory. On a conventional tail-last aircraft, the horizontal tail acts as a stabilizing surface by balancing the machine in flight with a downward force, much like the feathers of an arrow. The disadvantage of such an arrangement is that the wing already produces all the lift, and must produce even more to counteract the downward lift force of the tail. The more lift a wing produces, the more drag it creates. A 'tail' placed ahead of the wing actually contributes some lift while balancing the aircraft in pitch, relieving the wing of part of its task and making for a more efficient low-drag aircraft.

It is unlikely that the Wright brothers were aware of any of this when they installed the biplane 'front rudder' (elevator) ahead of the wings on their Flier. They saw the forward surfaces primarily as steering devices in the vertical plane, conveniently located ahead of the pilot to aid visual reference in pitch. The result was an aircraft which flew, but only just. The original Flier which made the historic flight at Kitty Hawk on 17 December 1903 was woefully unstable in pitch, flying in a series of divergent phugoidal swoops as described in Orville Wright's account of the flight:

'I found the control of the front rudder quite difficult on account of its being balanced too near the center and thus had a tendency to turn itself when started so that the rudder was turned too far on one side and then too far on the other. As a result, the machine would rise suddenly to about ten feet [3 m], and then as suddenly, dart for the ground. A sudden dart when out about 100 feet [30.5 m] from the end of the tracks ended the flight.'

Part of the trouble was pilot-induced pitch oscillation (overcontrolling), but Orville was also unaware of a dangerous peculiarity of the canard layout. He believed that the movable 'front rudder' could

'prevent nosedives'. Wind-tunnel experiments showed that the wing's centre of pressure moved forward with increased angle of incidence to a point where it suddenly reversed, causing these nosedives, which were actually stalls. The Wrights incorrectly imagined that having a forward-mounted elevator would prevent this happening. In fact just the opposite was true: the foreplane stalled first before the main wing, causing the nose to drop sharply and resulting in a loss of longitudinal stability.

Recent computer simulations of the Wright's control systems suggest that had they made the forward tail surface fixed, and moved the Flier's centre of gravity forward, the aircraft might well have been capable of flying 'hands-off'. As it was, the Flier was all but uncontrollable, which is a tribute to the piloting skills of the two Dayton bicycle builders, who later abandoned their 'front rudders'.

Design difficulties - and their rewards
Despite its deficiencies, the canard configuration can offer unrivalled safety and stability if, and it is a very big 'if', the canard surface can be designed so that it cannot stall before reaching its maximum trim position. If the canard does not stall the main wing cannot, resulting in an aircraft which is both stall- and spin-proof. Unfortunately the

Wilbur Wright lies at the controls of the Wright Flyer I after the brothers' first attempt at a powered flight on 14 December 1903. The Flyer I was a canard design, believed by the Wrights to ensure greater control, but the first flight ended in a dive into the sand of the Kill Devil Hills as a result of over-correction of the forward elevator by Wilbur.

balance between canard and wing stall progression is subtle and the 'design window' difficult to arrive at, which is why most aircraft have been 'tail-last'.

But back to the ducks. The Wrights exerted a tremendous influence on the early years of aviation, and many pioneers imitated their efforts with a spate of tail-first designs. In 1904 the expatriate Brazilian aviator Alberto Santos Dumont, who had so delighted Parisian society with his dirigible antics (*see Chapter 2*), visited the St Louis Exposition, there to meet Octave Chanute, who told him of the Wrights' progress. Here at last was news of real aerial conquest to tempt Santos away from his beloved airships. In January 1906 he announced that he would compete for the prize offered by industrialist Henri Deutsche de la Meurthe for the first 1-km (0.6-mile) circle flown in an aircraft.

Santos's entry was his *No. 14bis*, which was peculiar looking even by the standards of its day, with a 10-m (32.8-ft) span wing consisting of six box-kite cells joined in sharp dihedral. Another cell, which could be tilted up, down, or sideways for steering was mounted at the very front of the fuselage in canard configuration. Santos planned to fly the machine from a standing position just in front of the wing. His first tests were conducted in typically bizarre fashion. Santos rigged up a tightrope and pulley contraption from which he suspended the machine, then hired a donkey to tow it back and forth while he tested the controls. Alas, one donkey power proved inadequate for simulated flight, so he slung the aircraft beneath his *No. 14* airship and tried it that way, hence the aircraft's designation.

By now the dapper little Brazilian was also registered for two further prizes: the Coupe d'Aviation Ernest Archdeacon for the first aircraft flight of 25 m (82 ft), and the Aéro Club de France's 1500-franc purse for a flight of not less than 100 m (328 ft). He was clearly hedging his bets.

The first planned free flight on 21 August 1906 was disheartening. *No. 14bis* showed no inclination to leave the ground and during frantic dashes across the grass succeeded only in shattering its pusher propeller. On the next day the undercarriage collapsed during another abortive take-off run. Santos decided that lack of power was the problem, and so substituted a new eight-cylinder 50-hp Antoinette engine for the original 24-hp motor.

At 8 a.m. on 23 October 1906 Santos, immaculate as ever in striped shirt and bright red cravat, motored in his electric buggy to the cavalry riding ground at Bagatelle in the Bois de Boulogne. The hours passed with further frustrations, but at 4.45 p.m. *No. 14bis* left the ground 'like an infuriated grasshopper' and flew for about 60 m (197 ft) at a height of 3 to 5 m (10 to 16 ft), Santos all the while working at the control stick as if stirring a pudding. The precise distance flown was never measured. In their excitement, official observers from the Aero Club quite forgot their primary task. Three weeks later Santos flew 220 m (722 ft) and Paris went wild. Mothers named children after him, barmen their cocktails, and young men aped Santos's dandyish style of dress. But as for *No. 14bis,* it was a canard in both senses of the word, 'a monstrosity barely worthy of the term aeroplane' according to one historian. Though it had undoubtedly flown, it was horrendously unstable in pitch and was incapable of further useful development.

Blériot's misconception
Louis Blériot also dabbled with ducks. His Blériot V built in the spring of 1907 was one of the earliest monoplanes. It had its wings, foreplane and part of the fuselage covered with paper, and sat atop a pair of bicycle wheels. Blériot confided to his sympathetic and long-suffering wife that he had great faith in the canard configuration, but never did have his confidence rewarded: the Blériot V was wrecked on the very same site across which Santos Dumont's *No. 14bis* had lurched the previous year.

Several canards were tried in England, one of which (Horatio Barber's Aeronautical Syndicate Limited's Valkyrie B) became the first aircraft to transport aerial cargo in Britain on 4 July 1911, when it flew a box of lightbulbs from Shoreham to Hove in Sussex. That same year one H. S. Dixon built a 25-hp canard called the Dixon Nipper which would surely have been forgotten for ever had not the makers of the movie *Those Magnificent Men in Their Flying Machines* chosen to resurrect it as the mount for British comedian Tony Hancock. In the movie Hancock took off in his *Little Fiddler* and proceeded to fly backwards, seemingly fooled by the canard arrangement! The original Nipper was wrecked, which is hardly surprising, for it had no lateral control and the canard elevator was hinged along its trailing edge, so that any control input would have led to full deflection of the surface.

Two prominent aviation personalities succumbed to the attraction of canards during the late 1920s, one fatally. William Bushnell Stout, creator of the aircraft which led to the Ford Tri-Motor, built a freakish device powered by a pair of 32-hp Bristol Cherub engines. This had a large canard set very close to the main lifting surface, almost like the Flying Flea's tandem-wing arrangement. It featured the same corrugated skinning used on the Ford, a sort of Tin Duck forerunner of the Tin Goose.

Focke-Wulf *Flugzeugbau G.m.b.H.* also built a twin-engined canard in the same year of 1927. They called it the F.19 *Ente* (*Ente* in German means duck or hoax, just like *canard* in French), claiming that the tail-first configuration gave it 'exceptional stability and control at low speeds'. Stability and control in slow flight means safety, but unfortunately the *Ente*'s wing/canard relationship was not right, and it proved to be one of those many so-called 'safety' aircraft which was so safe it was positively lethal. It killed company founder Georg Wulf in a crash on 29 September 1927.

Apart from its low-drag and hard-won stability and controllability benefits, the canard configuration offers other advantages. The 'tail' surface is mounted clear of slipstream effects; engines can be located at the rear of the airframe, where they can turn pusher propellers without resorting to long driveshafts; and the configuration affords excellent pilot visibility. It was only a matter of time before someone recognized the value of canards to fighter design: a clean 'front end' devoid of propeller and engine makes an excellent gun-mounting platform.

A wasted opportunity

The first canard fighter design to appear came from Italy, where Ing. Sergio Stefanutti had gained some experience in the mid-1930s with a little two-seat tail-first tourer. His S.A.I. S.S.4 first flew on 1 May 1939, and displayed excellent characteristics during test flights. Apart from its primary role as an interceptor, plans were made for a dive-bomber variant. With a 960-hp Isotta Fraschini Asso XI 12-cylinder liquid-cooled engine, the S.S.4 was capable of a maximum speed of 540 kph (335 mph) at 5000 m (16,400 ft) and was to have been armed with two 20-mm and one 30-mm cannon, but while undergoing final tests at the Guidonia Test Establishment in 1941 it was wrecked in a forced landing after an engine failure, and although the Italian Air Ministry ordered another prototype, pressure of other projects caused the promising fighter to be abandoned.

Just as flight testing of Stefanutti's design had been getting under way, the American Curtiss-Wright company was working on a canard fighter design to meet a US Army specification. A development contract was awarded in June 1940, and Curtiss-Wright built a full-size flying-scale model of the aircraft designated Model 24-B, powered by a 275-hp Menasco engine. The Curtiss 24-B was not a true canard, in that it had no fixed forward 'tail' surface. Essentially it was a flying wing with a nose-mounted elevator. The 24-B made 169 flights from California's Muroc Dry Lake before a

contract for three XP-55 fighters was awarded. This aircraft, called the Ascender and known to Curtiss-Wright employees as the Ass-ender, a none too subtle pun on 'tail-first', was powered by a 1275-hp Allison V-1710-95 engine and carried four 12.7-mm (0.5-in) Colt Browning M2 machine-guns mounted in the nose-cone.

The first XP-55 was completed in July 1943 and soon had the area of its forward elevator surface increased to counter an excessively long take-off run. During stall tests on 15 November 1943 the Ascender flicked onto its back and stabilized in an inverted descent from which recovery proved impossible. All further stall testing on the other two XP-55s was forbidden until wingtip extensions were added, but despite

The Focke-Wulf F.19 *Ente* airborne during its brief flying career, which ended with a crash in which Georg Wulf lost his life. Most of the early experiments with canard aircraft served to illustrate that there were indeed benefits to the configuration, but that the dangers of even the slightest miscalculation were greater than on a conventional aircraft. The promise of canard aircraft is well shown in the caption attached to the original photograph: 'It can neither stall nor spin, and if it loses speed it simply sinks slowly to earth'.

or to be strictly accurate, tandem-wing air-craft. A tandem-wing configuration is one in which the foreplane or forward elevator is of approximately the same span as the main wing. During 1941 the British Fleet Air Arm had been having difficulty introducing shipborne versions of Spitfires and Hurricanes into carrier service. Low-time, inexperienced pilots were having trouble landing, and designer George Miles hit upon the idea of a tail-first aircraft which would give the pilot the best possible forward view for the precise business of landing on the pitching, heaving deck of an aircraft carrier. The advantage was twofold: having a double wing, the aircraft's span could be kept within the confines of the carrier's lift, thus avoiding the expense and weight of wing-folding mechanisms.

Nothing gets things moving like a war; in six weeks Miles had built a full-size flying test bed of his concept, the Miles M.35 Libellula. What is more, he built it secretly without the knowledge of Lord Beaverbrook's Ministry of Aircraft Production, which was supposed to approve all wartime work under pain of instant withdrawal of government-supplied raw materials and the equally swift demise of the company.

Miles' chief test pilot refused to fly the peculiar aircraft, so George Miles made the first test himself in May 1942. The Libellula proved catastrophically unstable in pitch; subsequently the aircraft was ballasted to improve its stability, but when the project was shown to ministry officials they told Miles: 'Don't be ridiculous, it will never fly.' When he pointed out that the aircraft had flown, they reprimanded him for building it without permission, while their Lordships of the Admiralty reminded him that in wartime lives had to be sacrificed, and they would go on wrecking their Spitfires and Hurricanes.

Another Libellula was built as a five-eighths scale model of a projected high-altitude, high-speed bomber and proved perfectly stable over a wide range of centre of gravity positions, but the bomber was never ordered because de Havilland's Mosquito was by then (1943) in full production. Nor were three other Miles tandem-wing projects ever to get off the drawing board — six- and eight-engined heavy bombers, and a triple-jet high-speed mailplane intended for British Overseas Airways Corporation.

Towards the end of World War II the Japanese also developed a canard fighter design which was the only such aircraft ever ordered into mass production. The machine was conceived in 1943 by Captain Masaoki Tsuruno, an Imperial Japanese Navy technical officer, who planned a jet-powered high-performance interceptor to counter the growing effectiveness of Ameri-

many modifications the aircraft's stall characteristics, particularly the complete lack of any pre-stall warning, remained unsatisfactory and involved excessive altitude loss during recovery. In other respects the Ascender performed adequately, though it was not equal to that of conventional fighters in production at the time and it too was abandoned. 'Its lack of stability and handling difficulties gave me the feeling of sitting astride a powder keg. I was glad to get it on the ground,' one Ascender test pilot remembers.

The Libellula concept
While Curtiss-Wright were having problems with their Ass-ender, the British Miles company began experimenting with canard,

can air power in the Pacific. Three glider
prototypes were built by the Dai Ichi
Kaigun Koku Gijitsusho (First Naval Air
Technical Arsenal). They performed well,
so in 1944 the Kyushu Hikoki company was
commissioned to finalize the interceptor
design. The Kyushu J7W *Shinden* (Magnificent Lightning) was a most revolutionary
aircraft, but instead of the jet envisaged by
Tsuruno, it was powered by the 2130-hp
Mitsubishi MK9D radial engine mounted
amidships driving a six-bladed pusher
propeller through a long transmission shaft.
It was armed with four 30-mm cannon and
with a projected maximum speed of 750
kph (466 mph) and a maximum operating
altitude of 12,000 m (39,370 ft) it might well
have been a formidable opponent. The
Japanese Navy ordered the *Shinden* into
mass production long before the first prototype was ready. Nakajima and Kyushu
tooled up for production of 150 aircraft per
month, but the first prototype did not fly
until 3 August 1945, a mere 12 days before
the Japanese surrender.

A technical triumph

The largest and most expensive canard
aircraft ever built was North American
Rockwell's XB-70 Valkyrie supersonic research aircraft, a mighty delta bomber of
which two prototypes were built. The XB-70
incorporated major advances in aerodynamics, structures and systems with the
aim of producing a bomber capable of
flying 9655 km (6000 miles) in three hours.
When the first prototype flew on 21 September 1964 it was simultaneously the
longest (56.4 m/185 ft), fastest (Mach 3 +),
most powerful and costliest aircraft ever
built, swallowing up $2000 million of US
taxpayers' money. Had it been made of
gold rather than advanced technology
metals, the 305-tonne (300-ton) Valkyrie
could scarcely have cost more. One of the
XB-70s was lost on 8 June 1966 in a spectacular accident when an F-104 Starfighter
formating on the immense white bomber for
publicity pictures was rolled by the Valkyrie's tip vortices and collided with it,
slicing off the Valkyrie's vertical stabilizer

Left : At the other extreme of size, weight, complexity and performance is the Aviafiber Canard-2 FL ultra-light sailplane of Swiss origin. This interesting design has its rear wing set in parasol fashion on top of the large V tail, and has an advanced structure of great strength but low weight. The first example flew in September 1977.

and sending it plunging out of control into the Mojave Desert.

The surviving XB-70 is now a museum piece, more expensive even than the world's greatest art treasures, but out at Mojave, where the second Valkyrie met its fiery end, there comes a mass revival of tail-first aircraft from a modest hangar marked Rutan Aircraft Factory. There Burt Rutan, a former flight test engineer with the United States Air Force, has developed a series of canard aircraft which have all the elusive benefits of the tail-first configuration with none of the failings.

Best known of these is his Vari-Eze, of which some 3000 sets of plans and kits have been sold to homebuilders (*see Chapter 15*), with more than 100 built. The Vari-Eze is an extraordinary machine, looking like a *Star Wars* interceptor. Its structure is made up from a plastic foam core overlaid with epoxy-glassfibre skinning, as smooth as alabaster. With a 100-hp engine it will cruise at 290 kph (180 mph) using no more fuel than a compact car, and the aircraft is truly stall- and spin-proof. Rutan has also built a prototype push-pull twin-engined canard called Defiant which does amazing things: if you shut down an engine at take-off and pull right back on the control column it just continues to climb out safely. In a conventional twin such a foolish action would almost certainly be fatal.

Rutan immodestly predicts that all twin-engined lightplanes will be canards before long. Perhaps he is overlooking the notorious conservatism of the aviation market, which has so far kept tails at the back end of aircraft, but the Rutan type of canard is no joke.

The Rutan Vari-Eze is a high-performance two-seat canard, with swept main wings of high aspect ratio. Designed for homebuilding, the Vari-Eze is nevertheless capable of a speed of 313 km/h (195 mph) on a 100-hp engine. A particularly interesting feature of this clean design is the fact that the nosewheel unit of the tricycle undercarriage retracts on the ground and in flight: on the ground this facilitates the hand-swinging of the propeller, and in the air it reduces drag.

Chapter 7
FLYING SAUCERS

For aesthetic as well as practical reasons, the 'flying saucer' or circular-winged aircraft has long attracted designers. As has so often proved the case, the problems associated with such aerodynamic oddities present their own difficulties, but their solution has been part of the designer's adventure, making the eventual success of men like Cloyd Snyder and Charles Zimmerman that much sweeter. Practical flying saucers enjoyed a limited golden age in the 1930s, 1940s and 1950s, but were held back by more conservatively minded manufacturers so that the saucers are once again the province of the visionary – or crank.

Above : The flying saucer is not, as some might imagine, a new concept, as indicated by this drawing of the annular-wing aircraft patented in 1895 by Estanislao Caballero de los Olivos.

Left : One of the most successful flying saucers was the Vought V-173, a flying full-scale model of the projected XF5U fighter.

'FLYING SAUCERS ARE real; airplanes are just an illusion' or so claims a bumper sticker favoured by Unidentified Flying Objects buffs in the United States.

It is true, in part. Saucer-shaped flying machines have been around for nearly a century, and were flying long before the first UFO sightings. One of the earliest was a disc-shaped navigable balloon devised by one John Buegger in 1888. Buegger's craft was powered by two engines and would have been launched along an inclined railway track had it ever flown. Seven years later a New Yorker named Estanislao Caballero de los Olivos filed patents for a flying saucer design which had a flat, circular wing mounted on top of an open 'bathrub' cabin. Two vertical-lift propellers were mounted in an opening in the wing, driven by 'the best obtainable type of engine'. The wing could be tilted fore and aft to climb or descend by hauling on ropes, rather like setting the sails of a ship. Like Buegger's balloon, Caballero's craft never flew, for which potential passengers should have been grateful, as sitting immediately beneath its revolving propellers would have been uncomfortably draughty.

By 1910 sufficient knowledge of aerodynamics, powerplants and airframe structures was available to enable any man of determination to build an aeroplane capable of flight, but some persistent eccentrics flew (figuratively at least) in the face of convention, and flying saucery caught on again during a craze for bizarre flying machines which followed rapidly behind the first years of successful powered flight.

Two English enthusiasts named Mortimer and Vaughan built a biplane with two pairs of semicircular wings which gave it the appearance of a double-decker ring doughnut. They called it 'The Safety', which was a misnomer if ever there was one, for the machine crashed and burned during its first trial at Edgware, Middlesex, in 1910. A second version proved safer, if no more successful, for it never flew at all, though Morton and Vaughan did have it photographed suspended on thin wires to give the impression of flight.

Another Englishman, G. J. A. Kitchen of Lancaster, patented a circular or annular wing and sold the rights to Cedric Lee, who built an annular-winged biplane powered by a 50-hp Gnome rotary engine in 1911. This 'Kitchen Doughnut' was wrecked by a gale during tests. Lee and his engineer Tilghman Richards continued to experiment with gliders and with wind-tunnel test models at the National Physical Laboratory and soon discovered that the circular wing had some very desirable properties. It continued to provide lift at extreme angles of incidence, and had a gentle stall. Furthermore, a round wing could have a span or diameter less than half that of a conventional surface of the same lifting area.

Annular wings

Lee and Richards built another aircraft, this time a monoplane with a conventional fuselage and tail surfaces and a 6.7-m (22-ft) diameter annular wing. The first flight on 23 November 1913 ended abruptly when the tail-heavy aircraft stalled an crashed into telegraph wires, fortunately without injury to pilot E. C. Gordon England. Rebuilt, the 80-hp Gnome-engined Lee-Richards An-

Even before Caballero devised his annular-wing craft, a slightly more practical flying machine had been designed by another American, John Buegger, in 1888. This was an attempt to produce a dirigible airship by turning the spherical gas holder of the balloon into a disc-shaped lifting body, from which was to be suspended a gondola for the crew. Propulsion was to be achieved by twin tractor propellers.

nular Monoplane proved easy to fly. With pilot and passenger aboard it would take-off at about 48 kph (30 mph) and had a maximum speed of 137 kph (85 mph). The original aircraft flew for 1028 hours during ten months of testing and was the first truly successful flying saucer. Two more Lee-Richards Annulars were built early in 1914 for the Gordon Bennett race, and after World War I Tilghman Richards tried to interest the Air Ministry in his unusual design, without success.

The inspiration for weird aircraft comes, not surprisingly, from the oddest places, but none less likely than a chiropodist's surgery in the town of South Bend, Indiana. There it was that on a spring day in 1926 Doctor Cloyd Snyder casually flipped a felt heel support across his office and marvelled at the way in which it skimmed through the air. Inspired by that most mundane of objects, he began to experiment with heel-shaped model aircraft wings and, like Lee and Richards before him, discovered that circular and semicircular wing sections possessed interesting properties. Not only did his models remain stable at extreme angles of attack, but they could even be made to pitch end-over-end and recover in level flight.

Snyder soon had visions of a huge 30.5-m (100-ft) span 'heel' plane, with a wing 4.57-m (15-ft) thick in which passengers would sit viewing the world through a clear plastic leading edge. He joined forces with woodwork students at a local high school to build a full-size glider prototype which one observer described as 'a mussel with a man in it'. The heel-shaped glider made its first flight in 1932 with a South Bend policeman at the controls and Snyder's family auto-mobile towing it on the end of a 61-m (200-ft) rope. The local officer's role as test pilot lasted for just one flight, whereupon Glen Doolittle, cousin of the famous Jimmy Doolittle, took over and flew the weird craft regularly throughout that summer.

Snyder needed two things to proceed with further development of his idea: an engine and money. A Henderson-Heath aero-engine solved the first problem, though its meagre 26 hp was barely adequate. To help with finance Snyder set up a stock company, the Monowing Corporation, and immediately laid plans for a second aircraft, which he called Arup – a phonetic combina-tion of 'air' and 'up' which he hoped would convey the machine's potential.

The second Arup was powered by a 36-hp Continental A-40 engine and had a 4.88-m (16-ft) span wing. To get aboard the aircraft its pilot had to clamber through a trap door let into the underside and crawl up into his seat, from where in flight he could look into the interior of the wing – a

disconcerting experience apparently, as the fabric covering seemed to be trying to pull away from the structure. This Arup flew very well, and its appearance coincided with a search by the US aviation authorities for a cheap 'flying flivver' to do for aviation what Henry Ford's Model T had done for automobiles. Snyder and Doolittle went off to Washington with the Arup and demobstrated it to the CAA, the National Advisory Committee for Aeronautics, the Army Air Force, the Navy Air Arm, even over the Washington Monument for the benefit of newsreel cameras.

Sabotage

A two-seater followed, with an 80-hp engine and a tricycle undercarriage. Doo-little flew it just once before a series of sabotage attempts cut short the test pro-gramme, culminating in a deliberately started fire at the company's new Indiana-polis hangar which destroyed the aircraft and most of the corporation's assets.

It looked like the end for Snyder's dream until a young flier from Detroit ordered an Arup and placed a substantial cash deposit. Though the money ran out when the aircraft was half-completed, the corporation persuaded suppliers to donate parts and materials. Number four was finished just in time to see its new owner go bankrupt, but its performance was im-pressive and on 25 May 1935 Doctor Snyder finally got to fly in one of his creations. As he and his new test pilot, Wilfred Brown, flew back towards the field the inexperienced doctor handed control over to Brown. At least, he thought he did, but when each man congratulated the other on his landing it transpired that the Arup had greased itself on to the runway. The big heel-shaped wing trapped air beneath it, enabling the aircraft to float along in ground effect, even at steep pitch angles, and then land itself. One sceptic challenged the Arup pilot, vowing that his conventional biplane could do the same; a collapsed under-carriage proved him wrong. The fourth Arup served its days as a flying billboard for the Sears-Roebuck company, for which purpose the Arup's generous wing area provided plenty of advertising space, and was used to carry publicity-conscious politi-cians during the 1935 Presidential cam-paign. Snyder's corporation collapsed dur-ing the Great Depression, and the two surviving flying saucers went for scrap during World War II.

Ironically, even as the Arups languished in the wake of the depression, a NACA designer and engineer named Charles H. Zimmerman was designing an aircraft of similar concept, but with a double-elliptical wing instead of the heel shape employed by

Trials with the Vought v-173 full-scale model proved highly successful, and Vought then devoted their full energies to the development of the xf5u-1. Although the programme was cancelled at the time of the first flight, there appears to be no reason why the xf5u-1 should not have been as successful as the v-173. There would in all probability have been some technical difficulties with the large articulated propellers, but these could have been solved. What is more difficult to explain, however, is the choice of a configuration notable for its stability as the basis for a fighter, which needs all the manoeuvrability the designer can give it.

Snyder. Again Zimmerman started out with models. His tests showed that with large-diameter propellers the aircraft would have sufficient thrust to take off and land near vertically and hover in flight, yet still be capable of high-speed dashes up to 805 kph (500 mph), far faster than any fighter aircraft of the time.

Zimmerman went to work for the Vought company, who patented the idea and presented plans to their number one customer, the United States Navy. Navy chiefs were impressed; they ordered a full-size flying model to be built to evaluate the flying characteristics of the proposed fighter, and this aircraft, the Vought v-173, made its first flight on 23 November 1942. The extraordinary-looking v-173 (unofficially dubbed Flying Pancake or Flying Flapjack according to taste) was constructed of wood with fabric covering, and had two 80-hp Continental engines driving a pair of huge 5.03-m (16½-ft) propellers. As with the Arup, pilot Boone Guyton had to climb aboard from below to sit in its pimple-like cockpit above the circular wing. The leading edge was glazed to aid forward and downward vision, thus realizing Doctor Snyder's 'window on the world' concept which he

planned for his passenger-carrying saucer.

The tiny engines of the v-173 were barely adequate, but the Flying Pancake took off in 15 m (50 ft), or much less with a steady wind, and could cruise at 222 kph (138 mph) despite its low power. Guyton and other pilots who flew the aircraft (including Charles Lindbergh) found it impossible to stall or spin, and full control could be maintained even at a 45-degree angle of attack. While the 'yellow pumpkin seed' continued its text flight program, work proceeded on two xf5u-1 fighter prototypes.

Complex but effective

Even the construction of Vought's Flapjack fighter was unconventional. To keep its weight low the company developed a composite material called Metalite, consisting of an aluminium skin laminated to a balsa wood core. The xf5u-1's engines were 1600-hp Pratt & Whitney R-2000-7 Twin Wasps, which drove a pair of 4.88-m (16-ft) four-blade propellers through a complex double right angle transmission system of shafts and gearboxes. The propeller blades were articulated and could be moved fore and aft on their shafts in the manner of a

helicopter's rotors, permitting the craft to 'hang' on its propellers in a semi-hover at low airspeed.

Vought's specification for the Flapjack called for a maximum speed of 811 kph (504 mph) at 6100 m (20,000 ft), while the landing speed was to be as low as 32 kph (20 mph). A proposed turbine-engined variant would have been even faster. The aircraft was to have been armed with six 12.7-mm (0.5-in) machine-guns or four 20-mm cannon, or two 454-kg (1000-lb) bombs.

The prototype XF5U-1 first began engine tests in August 1945, but it was not until 1947 that the articulating propellers became available and the grotesque Flying Flapjack began taxying trials at Vought's Stratford, Connecticut plant, though flight tests were to have been conducted from the United States Air Force Flight Test Center in the Mojave Desert.

On 17 March 1947, even as the Flapjack was charging down Stratford's runways, a cable arrived at the Vought factory: the US Navy had cancelled the programme in favour of jet-powered fighters, and the prototype, with its Bugs Bunny emblem on the nose, was to be destroyed. Rumour has it that during its taxi tests the Flapjack

briefly lifted off the runway. Certainly the aircraft had the last laugh, for when the breakers came, the steel ball with which they attempted to smash the Flapjack just bounced off its Metalite-skinned wing with scarcely a dent, and blow-torches had to be used to cut it apart. The scrap was sold for $6000, mainly for silver used in the propeller bearings. The V-173 fared better: it is stored at the National Air & Space Museum's Silver Hill workshop near Washington, D.C.

By coincidence (or was it?) a German farmer built a circular-winged aircraft during the war which was very similar to Charles Zimmerman's concept. The farmer, whose name goes unrecorded, apparently wanted to present the *Luftwaffe* with an entirely new type of aircraft – a 'flying beermat'. He had no technical knowledge but evidently was strong on enthusiasm, for single-handed he completed the aircraft during the second half of 1944 and persuaded a young *Oberleutnant* from a *Luftwaffe* unit stationed near his farm at Brandis, not far from Leipzig, to test fly the craft. It had a wing of about 4.6-m (15-ft) diameter, and was powered by a single 240-hp Argus inline engine. Like the Flying Flapjack, this *fliegende Pfannkuchen* got no further than taxiing, for a molehill damaged one of its undercarriage legs, the farmer failed to find a replacement, and the *Luftwaffe* never did get its revolutionary design, which may yet be sitting in some East German barn.

Promises, promises

Two decades after the wreckers' torches sent Vought's Flying Flapjack into oblivion there appeared in the American aviation press a series of advertisements for a futuristic private aircraft which looked not unlike Zimmerman's extraordinary fighter. It had a circular wing with two engines driving propellers through extension shafts, and had Doctor Snyder's see-through leading edge which gave all its passengers a front-row seat. Aero-Vista Corporation promised that their V-16 would cruise at 483 kph (300 mph), land at 64 kph (40 mph) and fly 4830 km (3000 miles) nonstop with six passengers and 454 kg (1000 lb) of baggage within its cavernous, pressurized wing. They offered franchise dealerships in the craft to all but established aircraft dealers, who would never have given it a second look anyway. Whether anyone ever did invest money in the project is uncertain, but if so they might have been wiser taking their dollars to the gaming tables just down the road from Aero-Vista's Las Vegas address, for the aeroplane has never appeared.

The Lee Richardses, Arups and Voughts were not true flying saucers. Rather they were aircraft with saucer-shaped wings. Credit for the invention of the first practical saucer goes to Doctor Henry Coanda, an expatriate Romanian scientist who will be remembered as one of the twentieth century's greatest inventors. Coanda's ever-prowling mind came up with the world's first jet aircraft (in 1910); a 1600-km (1000-mile) range strategic bomber in 1915; an early form of bazooka launcher; prefabricated houses; desalinization plants; and an artificial 'cow' with which he produced ready-to-use fertilizer for his château garden in France.

In 1935 he designed a Lenticular Aerodyne, which everyone else would call a flying saucer. It applied the principle of Coanda Effect – the tendency of moving fluids to adhere to and be deflected by an adjacent surface, an effect which one can demonstrate by holding the back of a spoon against a jet of tap water. The Coanda Effect has seen such diverse applications as agricultural sprayers, aerosol atomizers and jet engine thrust reversers. In his Lenticular Aerodyne Coanda planned to use it both to create lift and to control the craft's motion through the air, but he suffered from that perennial inventor's problem lack of funds and never built his saucer, which subsequent research has shown to have been perfectly feasible.

Perhaps not surprisingly, in view of its close and frustrating association with UFOs, the US Department of Defense financed development of its own flying saucer project in the 1950s. Avro Canada built the saucer for the United States Air Force. Called the VZ-9V Avrocar, it was powered by three Continental J69 turbine engines which drove a central lift fan with peripheral ducts and guide vanes providing directional thrust and control. The Avrocar was supposed to fly at speeds of over 483 kph (300 mph) at altitude and have a range of 1600 km (1000 miles), but the little bubble-topped saucer never exceeded 30.5 m (100 ft) during trials, which began at Avro's Malton Airfield near Toronto in December 1959. Despite the great secrecy surrounding the project, the Avrocar looked so much like the little runabout saucers used by the space-age Jetson family in American TV cartoons that few observers took it seriously.

From California, whence has come many a pie-in-the-sky project, came the Discojet, a diminutive 3.05-m (10-ft) saucer powered by eight Wankel snowmobile engines driving vectorable fans. Its two occupants sat beneath plexiglas bubbles. Discojet's publicity pictures circulated in 1976 showed a typically laid-back Californian couple about to go zipping away from their home as if having a flying saucer in the garage was the

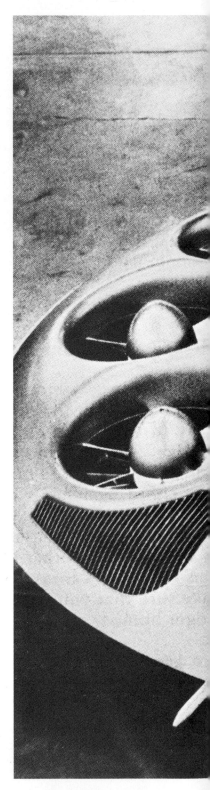

Above: Fact or fantasy? The Disco-jet was widely advertised in California, but as yet has failed to materialize even as a prototype.

Overleaf : Much was expected of the futuristic Avro Canada vz-9v Avrocar during the 1950s, but flight tests revealed that though the Avrocar flew tolerably well, its performance was at best only indifferent, especially in terms of its service ceiling.

most natural thing out of this world, but would-be saucerists are still waiting for production to begin.

Saucer airships

Personal flying saucers may still be some way off, but there is every prospect that saucer-shaped flying machines could operate public transport services before long. A major European car ferry operator has financed the development of the British Thermo-Skyship, a saucer-shaped airship using helium and super-heated air for lift and ducted thrust from turbofan engines for vertical take-off and landing and for cruise flight. A 9.14-m (30-ft) diameter model of the ship has flown, from which will be developed a Skyship car ferry capable of carrying 60 passengers and their cars from England to France at 165 kph (103 mph), and massive 152- and 508-tonne (150- and 500-ton) cargo-carrying saucers. It has been a long time coming, but the flying saucer may finally have arrived.

AV-7055

US ARMY

Chapter 8

PLANES THAT DRIVE, CARS THAT FLY

What could be a more attractive prospect than an aircraft from which the fuselage can be simply detached for use as a roadable car, or a car to which flying surfaces can be added to make a simple aircraft? The theory is fine, but as many would-be promoters have discovered, the development of a safe and cheap aerial car is very difficult.

Above: The Waterman Arrowbile was essentially a flying car version of his tailless 'Whatsit'.

Left: One of the notably more successful flying cars (or roadable aircraft if one prefers) is the Aerocar devised by Molt Taylor and developed through seven models.

REMEMBER IAN FLEMING's *Chitty-Chitty-Bang-Bang*, that marvellous, magical car which could sprout wings and fly? Pure fantasy, you might say, but this it most certainly was not. Within a few years of man's first faltering powered flights (and even before) inventors were dreaming, as they still do, of the ultimate personal vehicle – a flying machine that could be driven on the ground just like an automobile.

Glenn Curtiss, the great American aviation pioneer, was such a man. 'Now if we could just take off those wings and drive it down the street . . .' he would muse. No idle dreamer, Curtiss set to work in his Buffalo, New York, plant to build the world's first practical roadable aircraft.

The Curtiss Autoplane offered limousine luxury in its aluminium-bodied 'car': comfortable leather seats for an aerial chauffeur and two passengers, tasteful trimming in plush brocade, tapestries, even velvet drapes for the celluloid windows. Exactly how its triplane wings and outrigger-mounted tail unit detached for road use is not clear, but with a mass of rigging wires needing careful adjustment it can scarcely have been an easy or quick process. The 100-hp Curtiss OXX engine drove a four-blade pusher propeller by means of a shaft and chain mechanism. A clutch took care of power transmission to the road wheels.

The Curtiss Autoplane was ceremonially unveiled to an eager public at the New York Pan-American Aeronautical Exposition in Grand Central Palace, New York, on 8 February 1917. And what a stir it caused! Here at last was the machine everyone was waiting for. 'Prospective elopers get cue on how to escape from irate parents!', trumpeted the *Boston Transcript*. 'In it one can move comfortably along roads as well as through the gales of the upper world!' The *New York Evening Sun* was even more optimistic: 'Its luxurious accommodations are such as appeal to J. Stanley Smith of Martinsdale, a wealthy young sheep owner, who has announced that he will soar over the hills of Montana in search of his little black sheep,' it proclaimed excitedly.

Alas, the Autoplane was itself something of a black sheep. Poor J. Stanley never did get to soar after missing mutton in his flying shepherd's crook, for the machine only flew once or twice from the Atlantic Coast Aeronautical Station at Newport, Rhode Island, before America's entry into World War I intervened and curtailed further development in favour of weapons of war.

The two-engined approach

World War I also interrupted the work of Frenchman René Tampier, who had first discussed ideas for roadable aircraft with Wilbur Wright in 1909. He started up again after World War I and first drove his *Avion-Automobile* in October 1921. It flew two weeks later. Unlike Curtiss, Tampier opted for two separate powerplants: a small four-cylinder motor driving the vehicle's rear axle, and a massive 300-hp Hispano-Suiza V-12 aero-engine to get it airborne. Nor did Tampier mess with detachable flying surfaces: the biplane wings folded back alongside the fuselage for motoring. Between 1922 and 1925 Tampier built several different versions of the *Avion-Automobile*, all of which he drove and flew, but as a vehicle it was cumbersome and awkward and the idea was never adopted commercially.

The Auto-Aviator of 1900 reveals clearly that even a mere three years before the Wright brothers first flew, there were still many 'pioneers' who had totally failed to grasp the fundamentals of what was needed to make a heavier-than-air craft fly. And while the road portion of the Auto-Aviator seems to be workable, it is remarkably crude even by the standards of the time.

The Caudron-Renault company of Paris attacked the roadable aircraft problem from a different angle. Why bother with specialized, complex engineering, they reasoned with characteristic Gallic logic? Why not simply attach a road power unit to existing aircraft. An illustration in a 1934 issue of *L'Aéronautique* magazine suggested three possibilities: a tailless pusher-engined aircraft with a steerable, motorized nosewheel; an autogiro with a bolt-on supplementary road wheel; and the Caudron Aviocar, which was a standard Caudron low-wing monoplane with retractable road-drive installed in the rear fuselage. The scheme seemingly progressed no further than the yellowing pages of that magazine, which is perhaps as well. The rear-drive aeroplanes looked disastrously unstable for the cut and thrust of Parisian traffic.

If aircraft made poor automobiles, how about autogiros, those machines half aircraft and half helicopter which seemed to point the way of future aviation in the 1930s?

At the Berlin Light Aeroplane Exhibition in 1932, a full-scale mock-up of a proposed 'Aero-Auto' was displayed. 'A roomy cabin provides comfortable accommodation for four people,' ran the publicity brochure. 'The object of the "Aero-Auto" is to provide a general utility vehicle for the private owner, a machine which will be equally at home on the land or in the air. The pilot of an "Aero-Auto" running into bad weather or overtaken by darkness, makes for the nearest field or open space, lands, folds his wings [*which were actually rotor blades as we know them now*] and continues his journey by road independent of weather conditions. On everyday journeys no time is wasted on arrival at the aerodrome of destination in housing the machine or waiting for road transport. The drive is merely transferred to the road wheels and the "Aero-Auto" driven out of the airport to the owner's front door.'

The 'Aero-Auto' looked a neat piece of work, with an air-cooled diesel engine driving both the steerable front wheels and the rotor once it had windmilled up to take-off speed. Unlike contemporary autogiros, the 'Aero-Auto' was to have no propeller. 'The striking absence of an airscrew is accounted for by the presence of small upright wings fitted to the rotor,' its would-be manufacturers explained, 'and these provide the forward impetus to the machine . . . From the pilot's point of view the absence of an airscrew in the nose undoubtedly has much to recommend it.'

Doubtless pedestrians dodging the hoped-for thousands of 'Aero-Autos' on German streets would have appreciated that too, but the machine came to nothing, as did the Philadelphia-based Autogyro Corporation of America's Pitcairn AC-35, which became a familiar sight both on and over Pennsylvania highways in the mid-1930s. Extensive road and air testing of the Pitcairn was financed by the US Bureau of Air Commerce, who thought it might be employed on Philadelphia's autogiro-operated airborne mail service. The AC-35 was a two-seater with a 135-hp engine mounted behind the cabin driving a pair of propellers on a common shaft up front, while another shaft drove its single rear-mounted road wheel.

Not only was it ingenious, it actually worked quite well, but the Pitcairn AC-35 never went into production. In 1960 Skyway Engineering announced ambitious plans for mass production of a revamped AC-35, but like its predecessor, the project was stillborn.

The aerial car

Meanwhile, in California on the US west coast, Waldo Waterman was working on a roadable version of his *Whatsit* tailless craft (*see Chapter 5*). Waterman had worked with Glenn Curtiss on the Autoplane in his early days, and the notion of roadable aircraft had stuck with him. He took the engine from a 1937 Studebaker Commander 6 automobile and built around it a compact, two-seat, tricycle-wheeled car/fuselage of steel tube and aluminium alloy. The water-cooled 100-hp engine was mounted above the rear wheels, which it drove through chain belts for forward movement and a friction clutch in reverse, while a pusher propeller was driven via six vee-belts which were tightened for flight by a clutch pulley. He named his machine the Arrowbile, and to make it more attractive and familiar to non-flying drivers he further cannibalized the Studebaker for the dashboard, seats and steering wheel, the last of which hung from the roof and controlled the aircraft's wingtip-mounted elevons, rudders and the steerable nosewheel.

The Arrowbile's wings housed all the machine's control mechanisms and could be detached or hooked up for flight in just three minutes. During tests it performed splendidly, cruising at speeds in excess of 160 kph (100 mph) in the air and 72.5 kph (45 mph) on the ground. Could this be the long sought-after breakthrough? It seemed so, for along came the Studebaker Corporation with an offer to sell Arrowbiles through their dealer network at $3,000 apiece. Waterman set up a factory in Santa Monica and started building five examples for Studebaker's salesmen to demonstrate throughout the United States. Here at last was a roadable aircraft which the public could buy for a modest price at their local auto showrooms, and which could be serviced by any garage mechanic.

The Arrowbile euphoria faded with the 1938 recession. Waterman found that each aircraft planned to sell for $3,000 was costing him $7,000 to build, and Studebaker pulled out of the deal. Before another backer could be found the Japanese attacked Pearl Harbor, and it was not until 1948 that Waterman began work on his seventh, and final Arrowbile. He replaced the Studebaker engine with a six-cylinder air-cooled Franklin, renamed it Aerobile, and donated the craft to the Smithsonian Institution in Washington, D.C., where it remains.

The rotorborne concept

Although war brought American activity to a temporary halt, it inspired the most bizarre flying vehicle of all, and from the unlikeliest source: Great Britain, where interest in roadable aircraft had hitherto been restricted to lightplanes whose wings could be folded for towing behind cars.

Raoul Hafner, an Austrian expatriate engineer, was working for the British Airborne Forces Research Establishment when he hit upon the idea of using free-wheeling rotors to deliver airborne personnel into enemy territory. A controllable rotor would permit more accurate pinpointing than a conventional parachute. Having proved that his Rotochute (*see Chapter 9*) could support a combat-ready soldier, Hafner suggested that much heavier loads might also be delivered by rotor; a jeep, perhaps, or a truck, possibly a tank.

The scheme had a naive simplicity: take a vehicle, add a suitably-sized rotor and tail surfaces, tow it to altitude behind an aircraft, then cast it free at the planned landing point to flutter down sycamore-like for landing, after which the 'extras' could be discarded, allowing the vehicle to drive away. M.L. Aviation at White Waltham airfield in Berkshire were awarded a development contract for the first Rotabuggy, which appeared in 1943. The basic vehicle was a US Army Jeep, to which was attached a fuselage extension with a twin-finned tailplane, and a 14-m (46-ft) diameter rotor. The Jeep was equipped with a rotor control column which hung from the roof, a rotor tachometer, and a rudimentary set of flight instruments, but was otherwise quite standard. Preliminary tests were conducted with the Rotabuggy, or Rotajeep as it was otherwise known, ballasted with concrete to 1430 kg (3150 lb) and dropped from a height of about 2.1 m (7 ft) to test its impact absorption.

No problems were encountered, so a $4\frac{1}{2}$-litre super-charged Bentley sports car was hitched to the jeep and away the combination went, at speeds up to 105 kph (65 mph). By November 1943 the Rotajeep was ready for air-testing from Sherburn-in-Elmet airfield near the city of Leeds. An elderly Whitley bomber taxied out on to the run-

Below : In many ways the Waterman Arrowbile was an extremely modern concept for its time, and the more remarkable in that it apparently missed the failing that beset most other visionaries – general adequacy marred by one major, if not fatal, flaw.

way and took off, with a jeep in tow. The combination made one very short circuit, and when the Whitley touched down, the jeep, which had not been cast loose, remained airborne for some seconds a few feet above the runway. It was at this juncture that the bystanders realized that the occupants were unhappy. The pilot held the control column, which was directly connected with the rotor, while the driver sat beside him and held the steering wheel. Up and down, up and down it wandered, while all the witnesses stood and prayed that it would stall on a 'down' rather than an 'up'. This it fortunately did, landing hard on all four wheels, and the motor driver took over and steered it down the track. When it stopped, nobody got out for a while, and then the pilot was assisted out and laid out flat beside the runway to recover. Apparently the control column had whipped round and round in circles all the time they were in the air and only sheer strength had kept the jeep under control, so the poor pilot was completely exhausted.

Other test flights were made, and though the Rotajeep was officially classified as 'highly satisfactory', its instability problem was never solved. The development of heavy, vehicle-carrying assault gliders killed the project off, luckily, before an immense 47.25-m (155-ft) rotor could be tested on a Valentine tank. In the Rotajeep concept, wartime necessity had not so much mothered an invention as fathered a folly.

With the end of World War II, aircraft manufacturers, especially in the United States, deprived of contracts for fighters and bombers looked eagerly for new business. What the Americans needed, many of them decided, were personal aircraft for all those tens of thousands of returning war pilots to fly. So they went to it, preparing for a boom which never came. Scarcely a manufacturer did not come up with at least one lightplane design in the heady, carefree days following the end of war.

There were single-seaters, two-seaters, four-place family runabouts, amphibians and, of course, roadable aircraft, among whose champions was William Bushnell Stout, whose talent as a designer of automobiles and aircraft was matched by his P.T. Barnum-style ability at self-promotion. Back in the 1920s Stout, broke and down on his luck, wrote to every prominent industrialist in Detroit asking each to donate $1,000 towards the establishment of his aircraft company. In return he promised only that they would probably never see their money again. Stout soon found himself with $125,000, some of which came from Henry Ford, for whom he designed a moribund three-engined transport of clever construction and miserable performance which

eventually came good as the Ford Tri-Motor, though not before Stout and his patron had parted company.

The Spratt articulated wing

Stout's formula for successful aircraft design was 'simplicate and add more lightness'. To 'simplicate' his Skycar IV he called upon George Spratt, inventor of an articulated wing which could tilt in any direction to command movement in pitch, roll or yaw. Because the Spratt Wing (which George Spratt is developing to this day) eliminated all other control surfaces, Stout was able to design a stubby, compact fuselage/car body which looked like a giant beetle.

The Skycar was reportedly very easy to

Above: The Rotajeep concept, inspired by Raoul Hafner, had some considerable attractions at a time when the use of airborne forces was all the rage, but was marred by serious problems with stability and overall controllability.

A new approach to the idea of the flying car was pioneered by the ConvAircar, which featured a modular design, in which a basically standard car was sold to prospective operators, while Convair kept a large number of flight modules (flying surfaces and engine) for hire to owners who wished to take to the air.

fly, and took less than five minutes to prepare for road use. It was evaluated in 1946 by Consolidated Vultee (later Convair), who also bought rights to an original roadable design by their own Chief Development Engineer, Ted Hall. His creation was unusual in that the car portion looked exactly like a scaled-down conventional automobile of the period, though in flight, suspended beneath its self-contained 'flight module', it looked like nothing so much as a mouse in the grip of an aluminium hawk. The automobile had a streamlined glassfibre body with four seats, and was powered by a 26-hp Crosley car engine.

Where the ConvAircar also differed from previous roadables was that the company planned to sell only the car part, for $1500. Aircraft modules with 190-hp Lycoming aero-engines would be rented out by the hour or day when the owner wanted to go flying. Convair spent $800,000 on building two prototypes at their San Diego plant and gearing up for a planned production run of 160,000 ConvAircars. All went well until the third test flight, late in November 1947. Off went the ConvAircar with barely more than a whiff of gasoline fumes in its tanks. At worst it would have meant a walk back to the nearest fuel supply in a car; in a flying car it meant a swift return to earth. The ConvAircar ran out of fuel and was wrecked,

and shortly afterwards Convair ran out of enthusiasm, too.

The Flight Module approach was revived a quarter-century later by two Californians, Henry Smolinski and Harold Blake, who called themselves Advanced Vehicle Engineers Inc. AVE went even further than Convair, for they combined a standard US production automobile, a Ford Pinto, with the wings, tail and rear engine of Cessna's push-pull Skymaster aircraft as the Mizar. Even by Californian standards it made a weird sight. The Pinto was extensively and cunningly modified, so that its steering wheel not only steered on the ground, but operated the ailerons and elevators. A pair of retractable rudder pedals fitted beneath the fur-trimmed dashboard, which had a full panel of flight instruments and avionics alongside the usual Detroit fittings. Self-locking high-strength steel pins and tracking attached the flying surfaces to the car. Buyers were to be offered a choice of three modules with 235-, 260- or 300-hp engines, ranging in price from $12,319 to $22,974, plus $5974 for the Pinto, whitewall tires included. And if you were not a Ford fan, you could have a modified Chevrolet or Pontiac.

AVE's Mizar was surely the easiest aircraft ever to manoeuvre on the ground: you just shifted the automatic transmission to

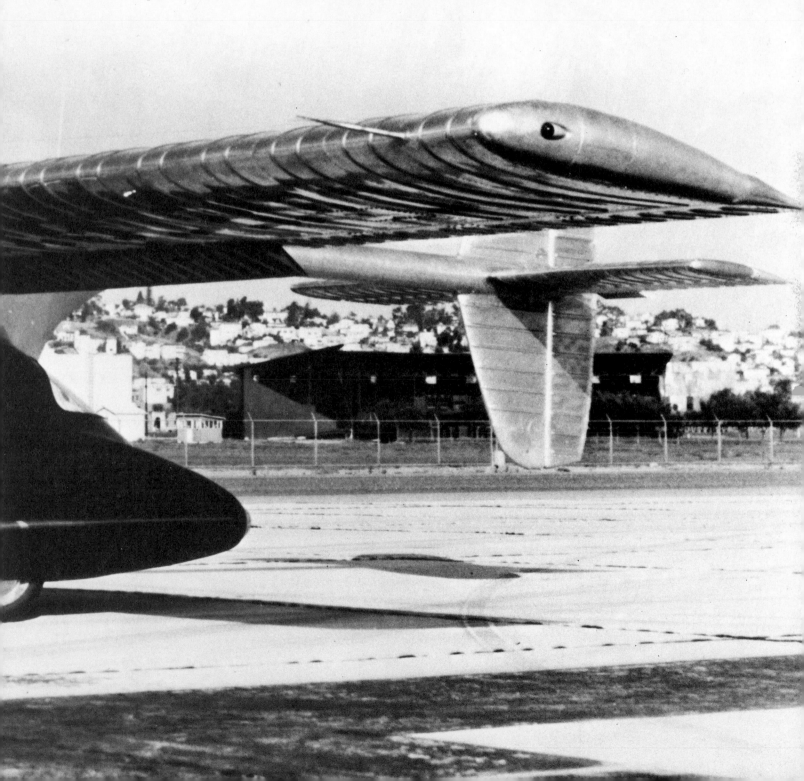

'Drive' and away you went. For take-off, the road drive and propeller could be used together for a swift departure, or so went the theory. In practice the Mizar performed miserably with a 210-hp engine. The powerplant failed on its first flight and Smolinski and Blake had to drive back to their airfield, which at least you could do with the Mizar. One day towards the end of 1973 car and aircraft went their separate ways just after take-off, killing the two inventors and their ambitious project.

Success at last

There has actually been a successful roadable aircraft, however, despite the previous catalogue of failures. Robert Edison Fulton, an engineer of Danbury, Connecticut grew frustrated with poor ground transportation at American airports and in 1946 built a roadable aircraft which entered production, albeit only in very limited numbers, as the first fully-licensed flying automobile in the United States. Fulton had a fine inventor's pedigree: he was a relative of Robert Fulton, the designer of the *Fulton's Folly* steamship, and of Thomas Edison. His Airphibian was a four-wheeled, two-seat, high-wing monoplane with a removable airframe which could be rolled away on its own retractable wheels after disconnection, leaving an aluminium-bodied soft-top coupé car.

Fulton used a 165-hp Franklin aero-engine for air and road drive, with auto-

Fulton announced in 1949 that he would build production versions for sale at $7000 to $9000 each. 'It flew fine,' a test-pilot reported during the Airphibian's certification trials, 'and it drove well, too, but it just didn't perform in the air because of all that weight and drag.' By 1950 the first three Airphibians had been driven over 322,000 km (200,000 miles) and made more than 6000 car/plane transformations. In all eight were built before Robert Fulton sold the rights to the design to private investors who never pursued it.

Then there is Molt Taylor, 'king' of the roadable aircraft set, who has built seven of his Aerocars and come closest of all to making the breakthrough into mass production. Taylor started out in 1948 with $50,000 capital put up by businessmen in his home town of Longview, Washington, where he still works. His Aerocars are unique in having fuselages, wings and tail units which can either be left at the airport or folded up into self-contained trailers for road towing. There is no point, says Taylor, in continuing a journey by road in the face of bad weather if you have to back-track later to collect your wings.

The Aerocar has been developed through three models, and although the last version, the Aerocar III, first flew in 1968 it still represents the proven state-of-the-art in roadable aircraft design. Taylor recalls:

'When we first started Aerocar and we first got it flying . . . I thought, gee, there's a lot of people going up and down the highway. I'm going to put a sign up there saying "When in Longview visit Aerocar, home of the flying automobile". I lie not to you when I tell you that next morning after we put up the signs there were so many cars parked down at our shop that there wasn't any place to park . . . I never got a damn thing done for three days. People came all day long and into the night to see the Flying Automobile.'

One can still see the Flying Automobile in Molt's shop in Longview: a small, streamlined red car about the size of a Honda Civic, with a pair of bucket seats, deep-pile carpet and a woodrim steering wheel. It has a 143-hp engine with a fluid drive system for its retractable road wheels and dry fluid drive for the pusher propeller mounted behind the aircraft's distinctive Y-shaped tail unit. In the air it will cruise at 217 kph (135 mph), at 97 kph (60 mph) on the road, and go 24 km (15 miles) for every 4.55 litres (1 gallon) of fuel burned, flying or driving. The seven Aerocars built have flown thousands of hours and driven hundreds of thousands of miles, but the crowds no longer steal Taylor's parking spot as they did in the days when he spent $4000 mailing replies resulting from the Aerocar's appearance on a single TV show,

The modular concept adopted by Convair also featured in the AVE Mizar, basically a Ford Pinto economy car modified to accept a flight module adapted from the wings, rear engine and tail surfaces of the Cessna Skymaster lightplane. The Mizar was very under-powered in the air, but this could have been remedied had not the two designers been killed when their Mizar came apart in the air during 1973.

matic hook-up of all flying controls. The aircraft's rudder pedals became brake and accelerator in the car, while landing lights doubled as headlamps. A safety device prevented the engine starting with the propeller installed unless all flying controls were connected and locked.

The airphibian was used extensively on business and pleasure trips. *Life* magazine published a photo story of a flying visit to the theatre by the Fultons, who flew 100 km (62 miles) from their Connecticut home to New York's La Guardia Airport at 180 kph (110 mph), unhitched the aircraft portion and drove across town to Broadway, all in less than an hour.

So successful was the Airphibian that

because his attempts to raise finance for production have been frustrated by bureaucracy. Taylor further recalls:

'Ford Motor Company wanted to build Aerocars, but the Federal Aviation Administration said no way did they want the sky full of flying automobiles, because if you put the flying automobiles out there you would soon clutter up the radar scopes and they couldn't tell airliners where to fly. That's too practical a vehicle and millions of people would want those. Ford would build them today if the government would give them any encouragement. Ford figured they could build a four-place Aerocar that . . . would sell in the price range of a Lincoln Continental. The Ford model had cantilever wings and four retractable wheels. It would be more than a Fiesta, more like the Pinto. They were going to build 25,000 of them the first year and with their dealer organization they figured they could sell them.'

It never happened. But will the day come when we will all be driving roadable aircraft and flying aerial automobiles? Molt Taylor believes it will happen. 'If it can't,' he says solemnly, 'then the whole of civilisation is dead,' though he allows that to put a flying automobile into production from scratch would cost $200 million today. Taylor puts it succinctly:

'Think of the vehicles that man has built: millions of automobiles, millions of boats, airplanes maybe a few hundred thousand, submarines with atomic engines that will go around the world three or four times on one loading of fuel, vehicles that go to the moon, but he can't build a vehicle that will go from your house to my house that will average more than 50 mph [80 kph] *except that one* [pointing to the Aerocar]. You wonder if it will get into production? It has to, because people will not be content with their present capability. The older I get the more convinced I get that I was right 25 years ago.'

This may well be the case. But on Molt Taylor's own admission, the proliferation of safety regulations and exhaust emission standards for automobiles in the United States and elsewhere seem likely to make future flying automobiles too heavy to fly and too expensive to become anything more than one-off curiosities. If you want a flying car, you will have to build it yourself . . . or discover the secret of *Chitty-Chitty-Bang-Bang*'s magic.

The most successful flying car to date has been the Taylor Aerocar. This features a compact car, which also serves as the main fuselage, and flying surfaces that can either be left at the airport, or folded up into a towable package so that the whole vehicle can be reassembled wherever the owner desires.

Chapter 9
GYRATIONS

Rotary-winged craft, which require little or no forward speed to generate lift, have many advantages over fixed-wing aircraft, most notably their ability to take-off and land vertically and so dispense with the massive runways needed by conventional aircraft. However, the technical problems associated with a powered rotor are formidable, and although the components of the problem had been solved individually, it was not until the advent of Igor Sikorsky's VS-300 in 1940 that the single-rotor helicopter became a fully practical proposition.

Above: To a certain extent the autogiro may be considered the hang-glider of the rotary-winged world. The example shown is the Sverchok-I designed and built by the students of the Kuybyshev Aviation Institute in the USSR in 1971 and 1972.

Left: With the Vought-Sikorsky VS-300, seen here in tethered flight with Igor Sikorsky at the controls, the single-rotor helicopter reached the stage of full practicability in May 1940.

AHELICOPTER IS A curious device, suspended beneath a whirling, flailing, barely visible means of support. In many respects the helicopter appears to embody both concept and technology originating after World War II, but evidence exists that helicopters were the earliest forms of flying machine, dating back 2000 years to China, where small two-bladed toys were made to rise into the air by means of a thread wrapped around a spindle. Such toys were common in Europe two centuries ago.

Leonardo da Vinci wrote in about the year 1500: 'I say that if this instrument made with a helix is well made, that is to say, of flaxen linen, of which one has closed the pores with starch, and is turned with great speed, the said helix is able to screw in the air, and to climb high.'

What better description of the helicopter principle, and what more logical than to adapt the Archimedian screw to auger its way into the sky?

But no-one did for three centuries after Leonardo. In 1784 a French naturalist named Launoy and an engineer, Bienvenu, built a large version of the Chinese toy. It had two feathered 'wings' each with a diameter of 71 cm (28 in), which contra-rotated from the power of a helically-wound bowstring. The device delighted the haughty members of the *Académie des Sciences* by swooping and fluttering around their meeting chamber.

Thirty years before this, the Russians claim, one of their men, Mikhail Vasilyevitch Lomonosov, flew a twin-rotor, clockwork-powered helicopter.

As in other fields of aeronautics, the nineteenth century brought forth a rare crop of vertical lift devices. Sir George Cayley, the 'father of British aeronautics' constructed several helicopter toys, one of which reportedly rose 27 m (90 ft); and another Englishman, W. H. Phillips, in 1842 flew a pilotless steam-driven rotary-winged craft which employed the advanced technique of ejecting high-pressure steam from nozzles at the tips of its rotor blades, just like rocket and ram-jet helicopters a century later. The Phillips craft was powered by a mixture of charcoal, nitre and gypsum, and flew across two fields.

One of the most fanciful projects was Frenchman Gabrielle de la Landelle's 1862 helicopter, which looked like a steamship with four concentrically mounted rotors on each of its two masts instead of sails. De la Landelle, whose major (and only) contribution to aeronautics seems to have been the coining of the word *aviateur* (aviator), interested Félix Tournachon, better known as the pioneer aerial photographer Nadar, in his machine, and to promote it together they

formed a society with the grandiose title *Société d'Encouragement pour la Navigation Aérienne du Moyens d'Appareils plus lourds que l'Air* (Society for the Encouragement of Aerial Navigation by Means of Heavier-than-air Craft).

Although de la Landelle's gross flying ship was never built, it almost certainly was the inspiration for Jules Verne's *Albatross* in *Clipper of the Clouds*, described here by her fictional commander, Robur: 'Well, gentlemen, do you believe in the possibility of aerial locomotion by machines heavier than air? You ask yourselves if this apparatus, so marvellously adapted for aerial locomotion, is susceptible of receiving greater speed. It is not worth while to conquer space if we cannot devour it. I wanted the air to be a solid support to me, and it is. I saw that to struggle against the wind I must be stronger than the wind, and I am. I had no need of sails to drive me, nor oars nor wheels to push me, nor rails to give me faster road. Air is what I wanted, that was all. Air surrounds me as water surrounds a submarine boat, and in it my propellers act like the screws of a steamer. That is how I solved the problem of aviation.'

No suitable engines

The real-life aviators were finding the problem more difficult to solve than did Robur, Conqueror of the Air, in Verne's 1887 tale. All kinds of powerplants were tried. J. Henry Smith, a student at Princeton, designed an

'observation helicopter' whose fan-shaped rotor was turned by two electric motors which drew their power from a boiler and electric generator on the ground via a long cable. Smith fancied that the device would be just the thing for sightseers; his drawing showed crinolined ladies taking the air from a cupola below the beating rotor, atop which was a parachute in case of a power cut. The Vicomte Ponton d'Amécourt built steam and clockwork-powered helicopter models which performed tolerably in 1863; Pomés de la Pauze employed gunpowder to drive his 1871 machine, while Castel in 1878 built a helicopter with eight rotors on two concentric shafts which were driven by compressed air through a tube running from the ground. The Italian Enrico Forlanini attempted to overcome the old problem of low thrust and heavy powerplants by pre-heating the boiler of his helicopter before attaching it to the machine, thus saving on fuel weight. His model rose to an altitude of 12.8 m (42 ft), still a long way from the globe-trottings of *Clipper of the Clouds*.

It was another Italian, one G. A. Crocco, who was to make the first real breakthrough towards controlled vertical flight since the ancient Chinese. Hitherto all the helicopter models and designs had concentrated on the problem of rising from the ground; little attention had been paid to the need to descend again, and none whatever to the problem of translating to forward flight – essential if the helicopter was to have any practical application. Crocco, who also invented the hydrofoil boat, patented a cyclic pitch control in 1906. In modern helicopters the cyclic pitch control alters the angular setting of each rotor blade as it meets the air, enabling the vertical lift rotor also to drive the machine forwards (or backwards or sideways) through the air in the horizontal plane, while the collective control alters the pitch of all blades simultaneously for climbing and descending. Without a cyclic control the airflow over the advancing blade, being faster than that over the retreating blade, would give uneven lift and roll the machine over.

Crocco's discovery that the pitch of each blade would need to be altered as it turned to balance the lift forces was perhaps the most important key to the development of successful helicopters, though he only identified the problem and failed to solve it.

Breguet's success
The first manned helicopter to make a successful ascent, though only with ground

assistance, took to the air at Douai in France on 19 September 1907. It was the creation of the brothers Louis and Jacques Breguet in association with Professor Charles Richet. They called it *Gyroplane*, and it looked like nothing more than a hastily assembled pop-art sculpture of steel ladders. Four biplane rotors giving 32 lifting surfaces were driven by a 40-hp Antoinette engine. Despite its weight, with pilot, of 577 kg (1273 lb), the *Gyroplane* rose 60 cm (2 ft) in the air, supported by four poles held by ground handlers, who dared not let go because the helicopter had no form of control save for an engine throttle. The *Gyroplane* was eventually damaged after crashing into a beetroot field, and Louis Breguet turned to fixed-wing craft, returning to helicopters only some 30 years later.

Meanwhile, working independently of the Breguets at Coquainvilliers, near Lisieux, Paul Cornu had built a more practical helicopter with fore-and-aft rotors driven by belts from a 24-hp Antoinette engine, which made a free flight lasting about 20 seconds on 13 November 1907. Cornu was unfortunate in that his flight came just as public hysteria was focusing on the fixed-wing achievements of the Wrights. He was unable to obtain support for developing his helicopter, but remained a passionate advocate of rotary-winged flight, writing *A Plea for the Direct Lifter* in 1911:

'The information available on the subject of vertical lift experiments is exceedingly fragmentary. Sufficient evidence exists, however, to show that the whole subject is of intense interest to all who have the real welfare of aeronautics at heart. The pity of it is that there should be a great number of cranks in the field. These optimistic and apparently harmless gentlemen do not assist the movement. They mix up ideas which have at least a basis of theoretical possibility with those which, like perpetual motion schemes, are obviously unmechanical and useless from their very inception. The engineering mind revolts at their weird conceptions and the suspicious capitalist is scared from assisting more reasonable experiments.'

Cornu would certainly have dismissed Joseph E. Bissell as a crank. Bissell, a Pittsburgh man, advertised in 1910 his 'Helicopter, Parachute and Gyroscope' which he claimed would be all things to all men. 'The arrangement possesses a number of very important advantages peculiar to itself which cannot be over-estimated by prospective aviators,' he proclaimed immodestly. 'The machine can be easily operated by a novice; it can be started up without regard to locality by a single operator; it cannot be upset; it will come down like a feather should anything go wrong with the engine, and should it alight on the water it will float right side up. In case of wreck the operator is less

apt to be injured in this machine than in any other because he cannot strike the ground until after the machine has first given way, thereby breaking the force of contact.'

One can at times sigh for the freedom which those early days, devoid of product liability and consumer protection laws, gave the intrepid inventor and charlatan!

Although in practical terms Cornu's contribution to rotary winged flight was small, he possessed a remarkable prescience of the future for helicopters, writing in 1911: 'The one pre-eminent advantage of direct-lift machines when they reach their practical stage will be their ability to hover. In addition to this they will be able to rise from any sort of ground and from confined spaces. From a military point of view, it is at once apparent that, for the purpose of taking observations, a machine which can retain its position for any considerable period must be more serviceable than one which can only remain even *near* that spot by careering in circles at 40 miles per hour [64 kph].' This is precisely the reason why, 70 years on, helicopters have ousted fixed-wing aircraft for

Just later than Louis Breguet was Paul Cornu, whose twin-rotor helicopter managed a free flight of some 20 seconds at the end of 1907. Visible in this overhead illustration is the belt drive, with power coming from a 24-hp Antoinette engine, for the two counter-rotating twin-blade rotors.

Oehmichen, who worked for the Peugeot automobile company. Oehmichen's first helicopter flew in 1922 for a distance of 60 m (197 ft). His *No. 2* machine was powered by a 120-hp Gnome rotary engine. It looked ridiculous, even grotesque, with four large rotors and eight stabilizing and steering propellers scattered seemingly at random about an open lattice-work frame; yet this was unimportant, for the machine flew. On 4 May 1924 this contraption made a closed-circuit flight of 1 km (0.62 mile) at Arlonans, remaining aloft for 14 minutes.

Cornu's 'optimistic and harmless' inventors were still around, even then. Consider, for example, Professor George de Bothezat, who fled Russia's October Revolution in 1917 for the United States (as did Igor Sikorsky, who built his first helicopter in 1909 and subsequently developed rotary-winged flight to the fine science for which his company is still famous). De Bothezat, an archetypal mad professor 'with mighty beard, spectacles, wildly excitable and constantly bad-tempered', badgered the US Army Air Service into giving him $20,000 with which to develop a colossal helicopter for which he made extravagant and wild claims, working in great secrecy at McCook field where pilots who overflew his workshop would be subject to fits of screaming pique lest they should have spotted what he was up to. His helicopter did eventually fly, and even managed to lift four men (three of whom were trying to keep it on the ground), but evidently failed to persuade the Army that they should capitalize on their investment, or tolerate more of his tantrums.

Little progress had been made when along came a handsome young Spaniard, Don Juan de la Cierva, who in 1919 had seen his magnificent 14-passenger transport aircraft destroyed by a reckless pilot when he stalled the machine in a low-level turn. Cierva determined to build an aircraft which could not stall and spin. Instead of adopting the vertical lift approach, Cierva took a conventional aircraft fuselage, complete with engine and tractor propeller, and installed a free-rotating wing. So long as the 'wing' or rotor revolved there would be sufficient airspeed to prevent it stalling. He called this craft an 'autogiro'; unlike a true helicopter, it could not take off or land vertically, nor could it hover in still air or move sideways. By the mid-1920s Cierva's success became known worldwide, and he was invited to Britain to demonstrate his machines to the Air Ministry. A year later a British Cierva Autogiro Company was established to manufacture the near-helicopters, early models of which were based on surplus Avro 504Ks.

Autogiro fever spread quickly. On 18 September 1928 a Cierva C8L Mark II was

army reconnaissance work and artillery spotting.

When Cornu wrote those auspicious words there was still a long way to go before controlled hovering flight became a possibility. During the last years of World War I a group of Austro-Hungarian engineers experimented with dozens of models and two full-size helicopters which were intended for military use as replacements for vulnerable hydrogen observation balloons. No other country conducted any helicopter research during World War I.

Full control at last

In 1919 the Marquis Raul Pateras de Pescara began trials with a series of helicopters leading to his 1924 biplane helicopter which had 16 rotor blades mounted co-axially with both cyclic and collective pitch control. He flew it in France rather than his native Argentina, succeeding in directing its flight at a speed around 8 kph (13 mph) and making auto-rotative descents with the blades free-wheeling.

Pescara's rival in France was Etienne

flown by its inventor from London to Paris with a passenger; that aircraft is preserved in the *Musée de l' Air*. British, French, German, American, Japanese and Russian companies built Cierva-type autogiros and no end of possibilities were foreseen for his 'wingless wonders', including traffic spotting, police work, commuting, mail delivering. In 1931 an American Pitcairn autogiro made a transcontinental flight. Cierva's final autogiro development was made in Britain, where in 1936 he installed a direct-drive system to the rotor: the craft's engine could thus be geared to pre-spin the blades, shortening the already modest take-off run. This technique was known as a 'jump start'. Poor *Señor* Cierva was killed in December of that year when the KLM airliner in which he was returning to his home in Spain crashed in fog at Croydon, near London, a tragic and ironic death for a man whom many predicted would kill himself in his 'whirlybirds'.

Autogiros saw limited military service during World War II. Cierva C-30A Rotas were used by the Royal Air Force as targets for radar calibration. In Germany a rotor-kite was devised for use aboard U-boats. The Focke-Achgelis Fa 330 *Bachstelze* (Wagtail) could be towed up behind the submarine to provide a high vantage point for spotting Allied convoys, the pilot/observer reporting back to the submarine's captain on a tele-phone link. Mission completed, the free-wheeling *Bachstelze* would then be reeled in, dismantled and stowed in a watertight, pressurized compartment on the deck. If the enemy shipping turned out to be a warship the submarine would immediately crash-dive, and the *Bachstelze* pilot was supposed to jettison the kite's rotors, which automatically deployed a parachute as they broke away, and ride down to the sea on its tubular fuselage frame, where presumably he either was taken prisoner or drowned.

By rotor to battle?

Raoul Hafner (*see Chapter 8*) came up with a similar concept – the Rotachute – which was supposed to be a better substitute for a parachute in delivering airborne troops to the battlefront, permitting more accurate descents and controlled landings. The Rotachute was first tested in October 1940 and continued in development for three years, making free descents after being towed to altitude behind Tiger Moths, but wartime events overtook the operational need both for this and Hafner's Rotajeep and Rotatank projects detailed in Chapter 8. One of the Rotachutes was shipped to the United States after the war; it led to Igor Bensen's gyro-glider design, which in turn preceded the popular Bensen Gyrocopter homebuilts which have kept the autogiro principle alive

Below : Unlike the helicopter, which is both lifted and propelled by its rotor, the autogiro is moved through the air in a conventional way, and supported by its freely turning rotor. Seen here is an example of the fully developed auto-giro of the Cierva type, a Rota Mark I of the Royal Air Force.

in sport flying (and in James Bond movies, in which rocket-equipped versions of British autogiro king Wing Commander Ken Wallis's machines have been used to devastating effect).

Whither the true helicopter in all this? Paradoxically the success of Cierva's autogiros spurred development of vertical-lift machines, notably in Germany and the United States, although Louis Breguet also reappeared on the scene with his twin-rotored *Gyroplane Laboratoire* in 1935, subsequently setting four world records in the following November when test pilot Maurice Claisse flew the craft at 98 kph (61 mph), to a height of 158 m (518 ft), over a distance of 43 km (27 miles), and for a duration of 62 minutes.

One year later, on 26 June 1936, Germany's first successful helicopter flew. Professor Heinrich Focke's Fa 61 was a true helicopter, though at first glance it looked much like Cierva's autogiros. Its nose-mounted 160-hp Siemens engine drove two outrigger-mounted three-blade rotors via gears and torque shafts; the propeller was merely for cooling. Crude, having been adapted from a Focke-Wulf Stieglitz trainer, the Fa 61 none the less proved more tractable than any previous vertical-lift aircraft. On the day before the first anniversary of its maiden flight, test pilot Edwald Rohlfs set

altitude and duration records of 2440 m (8002 ft) and 80 minutes 49 seconds. Next day he flew at 123 kph (76.15 mph) over 20 km (12.4 miles) and set a closed-circuit record of 80 km (49.7 miles). These records failed to gain much international publicity in the then current attitude of distrust of Nazi propaganda; what was needed was a sensational public demonstration of the Fa 61's capability. The wily Ernst Udet thought up a magnificent publicity stunt: he persuaded popular test pilot heroine Hanna Reitsch to fly the helicopter inside Berlin's vast *Deutschlandhalle* at the 1938 German Motor Show. It was a sensation. On 14 successive evenings *Flugkapitän* Reitsch demonstrated the machine in front of audiences of 20,000 people, including some very interested foreign military attaches. Later the Fa 61 set a height record of 3427 m (11,243 ft) which stood for many years.

Focke and Anton Flettner, who built his first helicopter in 1933, both developed rotary-winged aircraft during the war. These included the 1000-hp Fa 223 *Drache* (Kite) twin-rotor transport and utility helicopter, which was ordered by Deutsche Lufthansa in peacetime, and subsequently by the *Luftwaffe* who wanted 400 but received less than a dozen after Allied raids disrupted the production programme; and the Flettner Fl 282 *Kolibri* (Hummingbird),

Above: One of the main problems with the single-rotor helicopter is the need to counter the torque of this large turning body, such a counter-force usually being provided by a small anti-torque rotor mounted at the rear of a relatively long fuselage. An alternative to this is the use of twin main rotors: in a tandem configuration the rotors are located at the ends of a long fuselage, and turn in opposite directions; far more compact, however, is the type here exemplified by the Flettner Fl 282 *Kolibri*, in which the two main rotors are arranged side-by-side, angled slightly outwards, and arranged so as their counter-rotating blades intermesh without touching.

The best known autogiro of
modern times is undoubtedly
the dainty Wallis Autogyro,
seen here being flown 'hands
off' to demonstrate its stability.
This aircraft was used in the
James Bond epic film *You
Only Live Twice*, fitted with
a number of highly unlikely
weapons such as sophisticated
air-to-air missiles.

which used intermeshing 'eggbeater' rotors to eliminate torque effect (the tendency for a helicopter's fuselage to rotate in the opposite direction to its rotor unless stabilized by an anti-torque rotor at the rear, or by use of contra-rotating blades), and saw limited service aboard ships.

The true helicopter

In America, meanwhile, Igor Sikorsky restarted the experiments he had abandoned in Czarist Russia, patenting in 1931 what he termed a 'penny farthing' arrangement – a large main rotor with a tiny 'pinwheel' rotor at the back to neutralize torque effect. Practical application did not follow until September 1939 (mainly because of Sikorsky's commitments within the conglomerate United Aircraft Corporation with which Vought-Sikorsky had merged), when his vs-300 was ready for testing. The first successful flight was made on 13 May 1940 with Sikorsky, who insisted on test-flying his designs personally, at the controls, battered trilby clamped firmly on his head against the down-draught of the rotor. Within a year the vs-300 had surpassed the Focke-Achgelis's duration record with a flight of 1 hour 32 minutes 36 seconds.

Sikorsky's helicopter was still far from perfect. One service pilot who flew it remarked: 'More than anything else the vs-300 reminded me of a bucking bronco. She tried to throw me when she leaped into the air right at the start. When I wanted her to go down, she went up. When I tried to back her up, she persisted in going forward. About the only thing she was agreeable to was getting down again, and that was probably because she wanted to get fed and pampered by the mechanics and her maker.'

Helicopters are still tricky, maintenance-intensive beasts, requiring virtuoso performances on their controls to squeeze every bit of their remarkable capabilities out of them. Since Sikorsky's first tottering flights, undreamt of advances have been made, not least in sheer size. In 1948 the British Cierva Air Horse (which looked more like a mechanized clothes-horse) was the world's largest helicopter, weighing a then incredible 7620 kg (16,800 lb). The Russian Mil v-12, currently the largest rotary-winged craft, has a payload four times that.

In California the Lockheed Company is working with NASA on an X-wing helicopter whose rotors will be locked in forward flight permitting it to accelerate in level flight to transonic speeds but still hover and take-off vertically. And the bitter war in Vietnam proved that helicopters make fine gun-platforms, something which that clairvoyant inventor Paul Cornu foretold back in 1911 when his 'suspicious capitalists' wrote him off as another crank.

Chapter 10
STRAIGHT UP

The only solution to the problem of long runways other than rotary-winged craft is a 'conventional' aircraft capable of taking-off and landing vertically. Their dire straits in the closing stages of World War II persuaded the Germans to experiment fairly widely with such aircraft, most of which were suicidal in their operation, but did in turn convince the Americans of the possibility of VTOL fighters able to operate vertically thanks to their huge contra-rotating propellers. It was the British who discovered the optimum military solution, with the classic jet-powered Kestrel, while the more economical convertiplane and tilt-wing solutions are still attractive to the Americans.

Above : Another approach to VTOL flight is the tilting wing, here seen in a composite photograph of the Vought XC-142A in 1964.

Left : The Short SC.1 experimental aircraft was the first British VTOL aircraft, and was built in the late 1950s to test the feasibility of using a battery of jet engines (in this instance four Rolls-Royce RB.108s) thrusting directly downwards to achieve vertical lift.

A VISIT TO ANY major airport will soon make apparent the basic disadvantage of any conventional aircraft. Like heavily laden swans they need a long, straight run to accelerate to flying speed. So airports take up great areas of valuable land, with runways up to 5000 m (5470 yards) long, while departing and arriving aircraft cut a swath of noise across surrounding countryside which has residents rushing to form environmental protest groups. The attraction of a Vertical Take-Off and Landing (VTOL) aircraft, which can operate in limited space, free from constraints of concrete and complaint is equally obvious, but extremely difficult to achieve.

Helicopters are not the answer. As we have seen in the previous chapter, they have limitations; they are expensive to build and to maintain; their host of moving, high-stress components have short lives; they require greater piloting skills than fixed-wing aircraft; and in terms of weight and power helicopters perform less well than conventional types. The ultimate aircraft is one which can take off and land like a helicopter but perform in all other respects like a fixed-wing machine.

There are two fundamental approaches to VTOL flight. The aircraft can stand on its tail and thrust or bore its way into the sky; or it can be provided with a means of making it rise vertically, but in a horizontal attitude, before transitioning to forward flight: tail-sitting or flat-rising, in short.

The very first attempt at VTOL used the latter method, or would have done had it been successful. George Louis Outram Davidson began work at Taplow, Berkshire in 1896 on an idea for a VTOL airliner which he called the Gyropter. It was an ambitious project on which Davidson spent thousands of pounds and published hundreds of pamphlets and patents before settling for his final design which was under construction in 1911. The Gyropter had three sets of biplane wings between which were set a pair of 8.23-m (27-ft) umbrella-shaped fans driven by two 50-hp Stanley steam engines buried in its double-deck fuselage. These fans would provide the lift to get the 7100 kg (15,650 lb) monster off the ground, and could then be tilted for forward flight. This is the earliest known example of the concept for what is now called a convertiplane, though Sir George Cayley proposed a similar though less ambitious machine in 1843. Opinions vary as to the fate of the Davidson Gyropter: some say it was never completed, others that its engines blew up on the first test and wrecked it. Either way, Davidson would have had to be very clever to get 100 hp to lift a 7.1-tonne (7-ton) aircraft.

The convertiplane concept emerged again some 30 years later when another English-

man, L. E. Baynes, designed a tilting-rotor VTOL combat aircraft called the Heliplane. Basically a three-crew bomber with glazed nose and provision for a 227 kg (500 lb) bombload or other stores, the Heliplane had a tiny 6.1-m (20-ft) stub wing, at the tips of which were to be mounted gas turbine engines driving 4.57-m (15-ft) diameter propellers. The engine nacelles swivelled to the vertical for take-off and landing, and to horizontal for cruise, in which mode Baines predicted a top speed of 587 kph (365 mph). The Heliplane's fuselage would have been sealed so that it could also operate off water. Unfortunately this, and almost every other unorthodox project in the tense year of 1939, failed to get official approval.

In Germany Professor Focke and Gerd Achgelis, justifiably flushed with the success of their spectacular Fa 61 helicopter (see Chapter 9), also planned a convertiplane not unlike that of Baines, except that its twin piston engines drove pusher propellers and swivelled downwards in VTOL mode, pushing rather than pulling the aircraft aloft. Like the Heliplane, the Fa 269 of 1943 received low priority from the Reichsluftfahrtministerium (State Aviation Ministry) and was still-born.

A fiery adder

The final desperate years of the Third Reich also produced the first tail-sitter VTOLs in a last-ditch attempt to stop the destruction being wrought on German industry by Allied bombers. Erich Bachem's Ba 349 Natter (Viper) was a semi-expendable vertically-launched rocket interceptor which was incorporated into the Jägernotprogramm (Fighter Emergency Programme) in August 1944. It originated from proposals put forward by Werner von Braun for an interceptor capable of reaching the 7620 m (25,000 ft) plus operating altitudes of RAF and USAAF bomber formations in less than one minute. Initially the plan was that Natters would be launched at a bomber formation and attack it with a salvo of nose-mounted rocket projectiles. The pilots would then set up a ramming attack and eject just before impact. Early on it became obvious that the Natter's tiny fuselage could not accommodate an effective ejection seat, and that such a device would only serve to complicate a design which was supposed to be the very essence of simplicity.

The Natter's airframe was of wooden construction with a Walter 109 rocket motor similar to that used in the Messerschmitt Me 163 (see Chapter 5), supplemented by four externally-mounted solid-fuel booster rockets for vertical take-off. Armament consisted of a battery of 24 salvo-fired Henschel Hs 217 Föhn (Storm) missiles housed behind a jettisonable nose-cone. Unmanned vertical

An extreme concept for a VTOL aircraft was the Focke-Wulf *Triebflügel* design of World War II. This was to have been powered by three ramjets, located at the tips of the three rotating wings.

aircraft to stand vertically. Operationally, the pivoted wings would have been set to zero incidence for launching and the ramjets ignited after rocket starters had spun the wings up to high speed. By altering the incidence of the spinning wings the aircraft could be made to rise vertically and transition to level flight. It would have been a fearsome sight, the 840 kg (1852 lb) thrust Pabst ramjets making a ring of flame around the rotating wings. Focke-Wulf predicted a maximum speed of 1000 kph (621 mph) at altitude, and a rocket-like rate of climb of 7500 m (24,605 ft) per minute. One almost wishes they had had just a little more time in which to build the *Triebflügel*, just to see how (and if) it worked.

Strategically, as the Nazis knew, VTOL aircraft have tremendous advantages, being able to operate from almost anywhere with only a very small clear space. For in general runways are a tactical liability: one well-placed bomb can effectively knock out an entire strike-force without a single man or machine being touched. The Americans knew it, too, and in the post-war years when Joe McCarthy was predicting that Communist hordes would be pouring into free countries any day some fascinating VTOL projects were tried in the United States in an effort to turn any parking lot into a front-line defence base.

Tail-sitters

Two of these were not dissimilar to the *Triebflügel* in concept: the Convair XFY-1 'Pogo' and the Lockheed XFV-1 'Salmon', named after its test pilot Herman 'Fish' Salmon. Each aircraft was built for a US Navy programme, and each relied on the 5500-shp Allison XT40 coupled turboprop engine to bore into the sky, hanging on a pair of contra-rotating propellers.

The Pogo and Salmon get the author's vote as the most bizarre aircraft ever flown. The Convair had a broad delta wing and enormous ventral and dorsal fins, while the Lockheed had conventional wings with a cruciform tail whose fins were set at 45-degree angles to the wing. Both aircraft had little castoring wheels on their fins on which they stood, towering nearly 12.2 m (40 ft) above the ground, and wingtip weapon pods. The Pogo was equipped with a custom-fitted clamshell 'hangar' which locked around the aircraft and made it independent of airfield facilities so that it could literally be stationed anywhere the dastardly Reds might appear. It first flew, dangling from the gantry of a crane, on 1 August 1954, and in October made its first transition from free vertical to horizontal flight and back. The Salmon never did make a free vertical take-off. For early tests it was equipped with a spidery-legged undercarriage on which it rose con-

launchings of *Natters* began in December 1944; the first piloted flight took place on the last day of February 1945: with Lothar Siebert at its controls, the *Natter* left the launching rails but as it climbed away the cockpit canopy flew off and the *Natter* performed a half-loop at about 1500 m (4920 ft) before diving inverted into the ground. No final explanation of the accident was ever offered, but it seems possible that Siebert blacked-out from the *g* forces of the rocket launch. Manned flights continued, but only 36 of the 200 *Natters* ordered were completed, and the first operational aircraft, if one can thus call manned missiles, were captured on site by Allied tank crews before they could be tried in action. The *Natter* was not a true VTOL aircraft in as much as there was never any provision for landing it; the pilot had to bail out after making his attack.

The second Nazi tail-sitter was even more bizarre and without doubt the most radical project of the war. Focke-Wulf submitted in September 1944 a design for the *Triebflügel* (Thrust-Wing) target-defence interceptor which was to have a three-bladed rotating wing, set in the middle of the fuselage and driven by tip-mounted ramjet engines. The fuselage was highly streamlined; the pilot sat in a pressurized cockpit right at the nose behind a pair of 30-mm cannon. A cruciform tail was fitted with five wheels to permit the ventionally; the crucial transition to hovering flight was made just once.

Neither of the aircraft got beyond preliminary testing. The basic concept was sound; the problem lay in the extreme difficulty of landing the aircraft, even for aces like Salmon and Convair test pilot James 'Skeets' Coleman, who says of the Pogo: 'You couldn't slow it down – there was no [landing] gear or speed brakes or any drag producers . . . at flight idle the engine would drive you at 300 knots [555 kph/345 mph]. You had to use high-g turns until you got slow enough to pull the nose up. You had to make that transition as close to the ground as possible – right on the deck – or you'd zoom and gain too much altitude . . . To land, you had to look back over your shoulder, and depth perception is terrible that way. At more than 300 feet [91 m], you couldn't detect the onset of high rates of sink; it was a menace. If you came down at 10 or 20 feet per second [3.05 or 6.1 mps], it would tumble. You had aerodynamic controls only, and once you got vertical it was like a big pendulum, although the controls were very effective. I had trouble reaching the rudder, but you could roll it with the stick, which was easier to reach, even if you fell back in your seat . . . it would have been a pilot's nightmare.' Despite its limitations (imagine trying to land one on the pitching deck of an aircraft-carrier at sea) the Convair XFY-1 was the world's first true VTOL aircraft.

While Convair and Lockheed were experimenting with their US Navy fighter prototypes, California neighbours Ryan Aeronautical Corporation were flying a tail-sitting jet for the USAF with the same idea in mind – getting away from the vulnerable concentration of aircraft on airfields. Ryan's X-13 Vertijet was purely an experimental test-bed, a tiny delta which shot off vertically on the thrust of its Rolls-Royce Avon turbojet but had to be recovered by a tricky procedure of hooking on to a steel bar suspended from a truck-mounted gantry, after which the whole contraption could be lowered horizontally and driven away. One cynic apparently said after witnessing this performance: 'It would work. The enemy, doubled over with laughter, would be unable to get off a good shot.'

'Flying bedstead'

They would nearly have died laughing at a VTOL aircraft then being tested in England under the very apt name of Flying Bedstead, for that was precisely how it looked. The Bedstead, officially called a Thrust-Measuring Rig (TMR), was the brainchild of Doctor A. A. Griffith of Rolls-Royce. It was a flat riser which hovered on the deflected exhaust gases of two Rolls-Royce Nene jet engines like a ping-pong ball on a jet of water at a

Above left : The fantastic Convair XFY-1 'Pogo' is seen climbing vertically just after take-off, using the thrust of its two great contra-rotating propellers.

Left : The Short SC.1 VTOL aircraft was preceeded in the United Kingdom by the Rolls-Royce 'Flying Bedstead', a magnificent device to test the practicality of flight and control on reactive thrust with no aid from aerodynamic surfaces.

Above : The first practical VTOL aircraft in the world was the Hawker Siddeley P.1127 Kestrel, developed into the Harrier strike aircraft. The Harrier seen here is demonstrating its vertical take-off capabilities, with its four vectorable nozzles diverting the exhaust gases of the single Pegasus engine vertically down to secure reactive lift.

fairground shooting gallery. Compressed air nozzles provided directional control.

The data gathered during the Bedsteads' test programme in the mid-1950s led to the development of a special turbojet engine for jet-lift, the RB.108, five of which were installed in the Short SC.1 VTOL research craft, which made its first free vertical ascent on 25 October 1958. The SC.1 had four lift engines and a separate powerplant for forward flight.

The French also experimented with VTOL aircraft in the 1950s, beginning with the SNECMA Atar-Volant in 1954, which looked like a tail sitter but actually was a flat-riser, and the Zbrowski Coléoptère, which had an annular wing and looked like a jet-propelled biscuit barrel. This was to have been a prototype for a VTOL interceptor until the prototype was destroyed in a crash in 1959. The Mirage-based Dassault Balzac also adopted the separate lift/thrust engine concept and was capable of Mach 2 flight.

The dawn of practical VTOL flight with real operational capability came in 1960

when the first Hawker P.1127 V/STOL fighter prototype flew in Britain. A design by Sir Sydney Camm, creator of the lovely Fury between-wars biplane, the Hurricane, and post-war Hunter jet fighter, the P.1127 incorporated vectored thrust, which enabled one engine to do the job of lifting and propelling the aircraft by means of rotatable exhaust nozzles.

The production Harrier fighter which derived from the P.1127 is familiar the world over. Watching one perform is always an awe-inspiring experience of which even the most blasé never tire. Somehow the very notion of an aircraft which can pirouette and curtsy, hover, fly sideways and backwards then zip away in an instant, accelerating to near-supersonic speeds, is still hard to believe. But these it does, and a Harrier can even be made to move away rapidly in a lateral direction. Pilots call it 'VIFFing' (Vectoring In Forward Flight) and it is done by rotating the jet nozzles, thrusting the aircraft sideways through the air without turning, or decelerating rapidly, a valuable and

Left : The tilt-wing approach to VTOL is clearly demonstrated by the Canadair CL-84 experimental aircraft, whose wings, engines and large-diameter propellers swivel into the vertical position for VTOL, and move down to the horizontal position for transition to conventional flight.

Below : Another approach to VTOL is exemplified by the Bell XV-15, which has a conventional fuselage and flying surfaces, with rotatable powerplants and rotors at the wing tips. These act as lift rotors for VTOL, and then turn to the horizontal position to act as propellers for forward flight.

unique dogfighting technique.

What of the convertiplane? That is still not perfected, despite more than two decades of serious experimentation. As with VTOL jets, there are two approaches: it is possible to employ separate propellers/rotors for lift and forward flight; or it is feasible to arrange for the propellers/rotors (or even the entire wing) to tilt.

The earliest convertiplanes on both sides of the Atlantic were of the first kind. The Fairey Gyrodyne, which originated from a Cierva Autogiro Company (*see Chapter 9*) design, and its successor the Jet Gyrodyne had pusher propellers at the tips of stub wings, while the rotor was turned by compressed air nozzles at the blade-ends. From the Gyrodynes came the nearest aircraft yet to a VTOL airliner – the Fairey/Westland Rotodyne which first flew in November 1957 and set a rotary-winged world speed record on 5 January 1959 at 307 kph (191 mph) over a 100-km (62-mile) closed circuit. The Rotodyne, which technically was a compound helicopter rather than a true convertiplane, was powered by two 3000-shp Napier Eland turboprops, pressure jets driving the rotor blades. It had accommodation for 40 passengers and showed some promise as a city-centre transport (though incredibly noisy, and unlikely to appease the environmentalists, who were less active then), but it was

scrapped in a 1960 government-directed 'rationalization' of the British aircraft industry.

Current thinking

Bell, Curtiss-Wright, Hiller, McDonnell, and Vertol all built convertiplanes in the United States, as did a 'triumvirate' comprising Vought, Hiller and Ryan, whose four-engined XC-142 'tilting windmill' was one of the most successful of the breed, along with Canadair's CL-84 Dynavert. On both the XC-142 and the Dynavert the entire wing rotated through 90 degrees for transition to and from vertical flight.

The search for an efficient convertiplane continues. Bell Helicopter Textron are flying their latest tilt-rotor design, the XV-15, for a joint NASA/US Army research programme, and at the time of writing have succeeded in transitioning to horizontal flight and accelerating beyond 300 knots (555 kph/345 mph), which suggests that a propeller combination may have been found which works well in both modes. Hitherto practical limitations on diameter have produced propellers too big to be efficient in cruise flight, and too small as rotors for lift-off and hovering: the worst combination in an aircraft type which when perfected, as it surely will be, should provide the best of all possible worlds.

Chapter 11

A PLANE IN YOUR SUITCASE

The concept of an aircraft which can be packed up when not in use is highly attractive, especially for emergency use. But such craft must always be limited in performance, and although the Americans at times felt that the strap-on rocket belt offered possibilities, the fold-away aircraft seems restricted to 'fun fliers'.

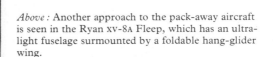

Above : Another approach to the pack-away aircraft is seen in the Ryan XV-8A Fleep, which has an ultra-light fuselage surmounted by a foldable hang-glider wing.

Left : The two crew members of the US Army look well pleased with the performance of the Goodyear Inflatobird, but the type was ultimately rejected.

PICTURE THE SCENE: a station wagon draws up at an airport, and out get two men carrying a long cylinder from which they extract a crumpled bundle of olive-drab rubberized fabric looking, when laid out on the grass, like a monstrous, aircraft-shaped balloon to which someone has taken a sharp pin; the men connect up a small air pump and the result is instant aircraft!

This absurd scenario, worthy of the *Monty Python's Flying Circus* team at its zany best, comes courtesy of the Goodyear Tyre and Rubber Company of Akron, Ohio, and it is no joke. Goodyear developed their Inflatobird pack-a-plane during the 1950s for the US Army.

The idea was that the Inflatobird would serve as a cheap infantry-portable reconnaissance aircraft, a remotely-piloted drone (when you hear the hiss you know you have scored a direct hit), or as a parachute-dropped escape craft for pilots downed in enemy territory. A conventional aircraft would drop the Inflatobird's 2.13- by 0.91-m (7- by 3-ft) container and, assuming he could get the air pump started or had strong lungs, the stranded flier could be on his way again in six minutes, escaping his captors with a quick leap and a bound.

Goodyear's flying airbed was made of rubberized nylon with drop threads and guy wires to maintain its aerodynamic shape once inflated. Puffed up it looked very much like an ordinary aircraft, with open cockpits for two occupants and a pylon-mounted 60-hp engine which gave it a 111-kph (70-mph) cruising speed with over five hours' duration of $16\frac{1}{2}$ Imperial gallons (75 litres) of fuel, all included in the pack.

The US Army was not ready for blow-up aircraft, however, and civilian certification standards prevented Goodyear from offering their Inflatobird to an eager public. Imagine the convenience of an aircraft which one could land like thistledown (taking care not to bounce or one might go bouncing on for ever) then roll up and store in a closet.

The British company M. L. Aviation, who built the wartime Rotajeep (*see Chapter 8*) also experimented with inflatable aircraft. Like the Inflatobird, their craft was intended as a cheap utility machine for the military. Unlike the almost conventional-looking Goodyear creation, the M.L. Utility had a large crescent-shaped blow-up wing, with no fuselage or tail. Its two crew sat in an open nacelle slung underneath. This craft could also be packed in a small container. Its 50-hp Walter Mikron engine pushed it along at an unhurried 72 kph (45 mph) and would get it off the ground at no more than 32 kph (20 mph) in even the lightest breeze.

Like their Pentagon counterparts, the British army's authorities were unimpressed.

The Goodyear Inflatobird begins to take shape as the small compressor, operated by the man in the striped shirt, feeds air into the rubberized fabric aircraft. Plainly visible are the four-cylinder air-cooled engine, driving a two-blade propeller, and the four landing wires running from the engine pylon to points about two-thirds of the way along each wing. These hold the wing up as the aircraft lands, while complementary wires from the bottom of the fuselage run up to the under surfaces of the wing to ensure that the wing does not buckle up in flight.

Shortly after World War II American generals were overtaken by a craze for tiny helicopters, aboard which their infantrymen were to go fluttering into battle like angry sycamore seeds. One such was the Hoppi-copter, which weighed just 41 kg (90 lb) and was strapped directly to the GI's back. It had a 20-hp engine and co-axial rotor blades of 3.66-m (12-ft) diameter. Unfortunately the landing gear – GIS' legs – proved inadequate for the shocks of touchdown and the scheme was shelved.

Strap-on helicopter

Perhaps modern soldiers' limbs are tougher, for the idea resurfaced in 1973. Aerospace General Corporation of Odessa, Texas announced their Mini-Copter, which revived the back-pack 'chopper' concept, this time with an optional landing skid for the weak-kneed. There was talk of a possible civilian version which would sell, as such things always do, for the price of the proverbial small car. One enthusiastic reporter, cheered by good Texan hospitality, predicted that housewives would go out for a loaf of bread, flying door-to-store by rocket-powered strap-on whirlybird.

Two tiny rocket motors the size of a cigarette pack powered the Mini-Copter, converting hydrogen peroxide fuel into superheated steam which was released through rotor-tip nozzles, providing power equivalent to a 90-hp engine. Fuel was carried in two briefcase-sized tanks each side of the pilot, and the entire machine fitted into a cylindrical container no larger than a jet fighter's droptank. At the last count the Mini-Copter was still in (slow) development, and presumably Texas housewives are still driving to the supermarket for their daily bread.

The smallest pack-away flying machines and the closest technology has yet to come to levitation were Bell Aerosystems Rocket Belts. These extraordinary strap-on devices had a pair of vectorable nozzles controlled by handlebars and enabled the wearer to go leaping over obstacles with mighty rocket-propelled footsteps. Hills, rivers, fortifications and similar inconveniences were no hindrance to the man with a rocket belt, which could thrust him up and over a 15-m (50-ft) tree like a ping-pong ball on a fair-ground water jet. To date the only practical application of the Rocket Belt on earth has been as a gimmick in a James Bond movie, but developed versions of the device have been used by NASA astronauts for space-walking and will be employed by crew-members on the Space Shuttle programme.

Although the military have shunned pack-away aircraft, the potential demand among private fliers is high. John Nicolaides, an

Perhaps one of the more extreme measures considered to achieve lightweight vertical flight is the rocket belt devised by Bell Aero-systems. Neat and potentially useful, the rocket belt has proved difficult to control with the finesse necessary for everyday use by non-experts.

aeronautical engineer from San Luis Obispo, California, spends some time each day returning unsolicited money from customers begging for one of his parafoil-wing aircraft. Nicolaides' craft looks like a go-cart dangling beneath an air-mattress and was inspired by an ancient Chinese multi-cell boxkite. The parafoil wing works on the same principle as the ram-air steerable parachutes used by advanced skydivers: forward motion forces air into the open front of the parafoil and inflates its cells to an airfoil shape, which has all the properties (and more) of a conventional aircraft wing. The parafoil is made of high-strength rip-stop nylon sailcloth. A cat's cradle of supporting lines distributes the airload. To prove its strength Nicolaides once had a parafoil wing shot up by gunners on an army range, then flew away.

Nicolaides maintains that the parafoil aircraft is simple to fly. There are just two controls: a rudder bar for left and right and a throttle to go up or down. Speed is 40 kph (25 mph), and the machine cannot be stalled because airspeed and angle of attack are constant. The landing run is a mere 3 m (10 ft). There is but one problem: the machines are not yet for sale. Nicolaides estimates that a production version with a converted snowmobile engine could be marketed at motorcycle prices, about $1500. For a few thousand dollars more he says he could develop a roadable version that could be driven or flown.

The cheap, slow-flying, highly manoeuvrable Nicolaides parafoils could replace expensive, maintenance-intensive helicopters for police, traffic and military surveillance work; or land directly on post office roofs for mail deliveries; or deliver men and equipment to remote sites (a version with a payload of 5080 kg/11,200 lb has already been built, or rather sewn); or even serve as motorized parachutes for ejecting pilots. Production versions would come neatly packed in a pair of matching suitcases, Nicolaides promises.

Powered hang-gliders

The future for pack-away craft is good. Ultralight aircraft which originated among American hang-glider enthusiasts who could not resist the temptation to add a little horsepower to their kites are rapidly gaining popularity, and may yet bring to fruition the dream of everyman's flying machine, so long sought after but never quite achieved by successive generations of designers and manufacturers.

The simplest ultralights are little more than Rogallo hang-gliders adapted to take a 10-hp chainsaw engine, driving an extension shaft, and pusher propeller situated just behind the prone pilot's ankles. More sophisticated machines feature semi-rigid construction of very light alloys or modern composite materials with ripstop nylon or plastic film covering, and have either weight-shift or full aerodynamic controls. Such ultralights are capable of surprising perfor-

mance, with speeds in the 80-kph (50-mph) range and exceedingly meagre field requirements, so that any small pasture can become an 'airport'. At the time of writing ultralights fall outside the certification and licensing requirements of most of the world's civil aviation bodies, which means they can be flown without a pilot's licence, but the increasing capability of these machines, which have flown the English Channel and made cross-country flights of several hundred miles, seem certain to attract regulatory attention in time.

Meanwhile, although a typical ultralight will not fit into a suitcase, they are easily portable on top of a car, and at $2000 or $3000 each are the cheapest powered flying machines on the market. They also constitute the fastest-growing sector of flying.

Chapter 12
HITCHING A RIDE

Aircraft designers are unavoidably caught in a cleft stick: aircraft with good performance in range must inevitably be large, weighty and so handicapped in other aspects of performance; while high-performance aircraft must be relatively small and light, and therefore incapable of great range. But the need, largely found by the military, for a high-performance aircraft capable of operating at long range led to a number of experiments with parasite aircraft: these craft, normally fighters, were carried in larger machines which acted as airborne aircraft-carriers.

Left : The space shuttle *Enterprise* lifts off a modified Boeing 747 for a gliding test flight.

Above : At the other extreme of the size spectrum was the diminutive McDonnell XF-85 Goblin parasite fighter, designed for carriage by the mighty Convair B-36 bomber.

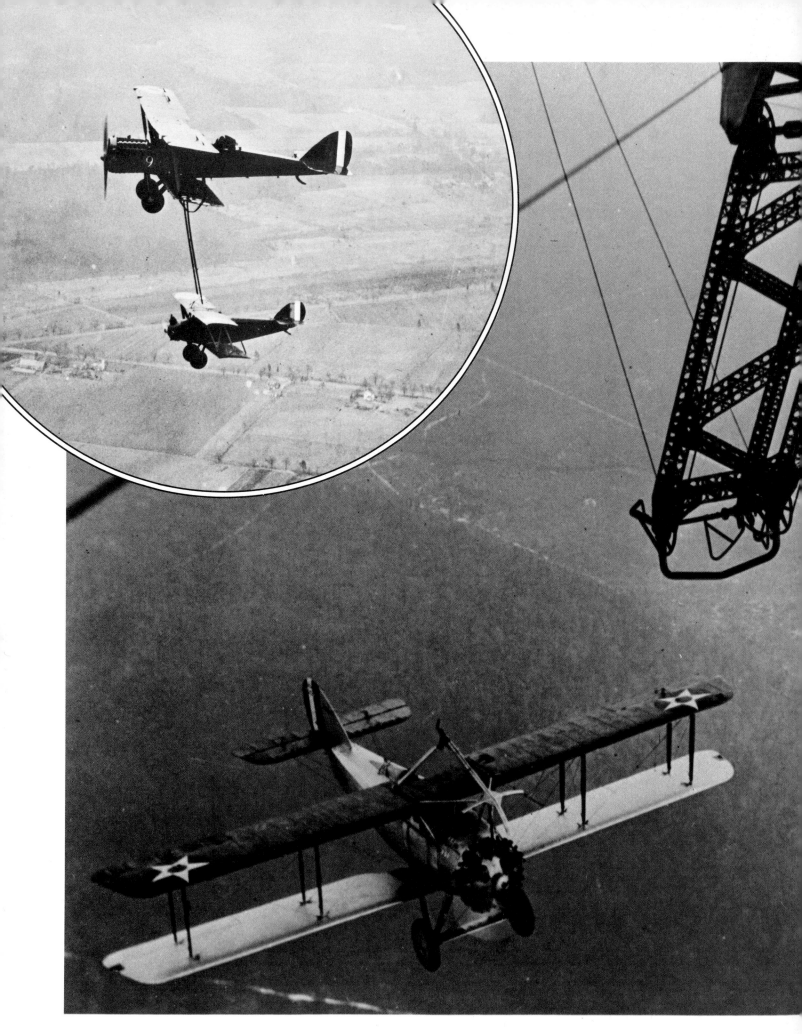

STROLLERS ALONG THE shore at Felixstowe, Suffolk on England's east coast were treated to a bizarre spectacle on 17 May 1916. From the nearby Royal Naval Service seaplane base there arose a Felixstowe Baby tri-motor flying-boat, on top of which was mounted a Bristol Scout C fighter. It was the first experiment in composite or 'pick-a-back' aircraft. The purpose of this weird duo was to investigate the possibility of limited-range scout (as fighters were then called) aircraft being ferried aloft by larger machines to patrol the coastline looking for raiding Zeppelin airships. Once the enemy was sighted the scout could then be released to make an attack and return to base normally. On this occasion the Bristol piloted by Flight Lieutenant M. J. Day, separated successfully from the Felixstowe at 305 m (1000 ft) over the town of Harwich and climbed away, returning to its land base at Martlesham Heath uneventfully.

Aerial hitch-hiking was not entirely new even then. Birdmen Jacob Degen, Vincent de Groof (*see Chapter 1*) and others used balloons to hoist themselves aloft for gliding descents, and though he never intended to cast off, Alberto Santos Dumont suspended his *No. 14bis* aircraft from a balloon to try out its control responses in 1906.

Although the Felixstowe trial had been modestly successful, it was to lighter-than-air craft that the experimenters turned once again in the search for a practical airborne aircraft-carrier. The disadvantage of the Felixstowe Baby/Bristol Scout combination had been that the Scout was forced to return to land; no one at the time seriously considered an air-to-air mating between two aircraft – a sure recipe for disaster. An airship offered greater possibilities, however.

Trials began in July 1918 with a Sopwith Camel fighter modified to incorporate Little Crook gear, which had nothing to do with petty criminals, but was a quick-release attachment devised by Major I. C. Little and Captain E. Crook of No. 212 Squadron, Royal Air Force. The 'aircraft carrier' was His Majesty's Airship *R23*. On 3 November 1918 the first release was made, using a pilotless Camel with locked control surfaces; it detached cleanly and glided back to earth. Another Camel was then rigged up, this time with No. 212's Lieutenant R. E. Keys aboard, and he too dropped away from the ship without incident, started the Camel's engines and circled *R23* before flying back to Pulham Airship Station in Norfolk.

The end of World War I slowed the pace of developments, so that it was not until February 1921 that the first attempt was made to retrieve the Camel after launching using an overhead wire-catcher to hook onto the mother ship. Further trials were carried out in 1925 using the airship *R33* and a pair of modified de Havilland D.H. 53 Humming Bird lightplanes suspended from a trapeze device beneath the ship. On 15 October 1925 Squadron Leader R. de Haga Haig climbed into the Humming Bird's cockpit at 1160 m (3800 ft) swung clear of the airship's hull on the trapeze and cast off, performing two loops before rejoining the carrier. Further flights were made with Gloster Grebe fighters.

Much the same kind of experimenting was going on in the United States. There the US Army conducted trials with a tiny Sperry Messenger biplane in 1924, but the US Navy, then championing the rigid airship for long-range ocean patrol, planned to use standard service aircraft from airships and commissioned the Goodyear-Zeppelin company to install a trapeze mounting aboard the 200-m (658-ft) long *Los Angeles*.

The trapeze was a stout girder structure with a bar at the bottom which could be lowered 7.62 m (25 ft) below the airship's hull for launching, and winched back up when the aircraft was safely returned. The first successful hook-up was made by a Vought UO-1 Aztec two-seat biplane on 3 July 1929, using a hook mounted above the upper wing on a braced mount which incorporated a deflector strip to guide the trapeze bar into the open jaws of the hook.

Airborne aircraft-carriers

The ultimate aim of the US Navy's experiments was to perfect a launching and retrieval technique for its two giant sisterships *Akron* and *Macon*, which were each to carry five fighter aircraft in an internal hangar. But before either was commissioned, Admiral William Moffett, the first chief of the Navy's Bureau of Aeronautics, proposed an even odder use for the aerial trapeze. Mindful of the problems of handling big airships during off-base landings, Moffett suggested that every ship might carry a small glider in which a skilled landing officer could glide down ahead of the airship and organize a handling crew for its arrival. Pioneer aviator Ralph Barnaby made a test from *Los Angeles* in a Prüfling glider on 31 January 1930, at Lakehurst, New Jersey:

'We went down the coast to Atlantic City and then came back in at 3000 feet [914 m]. When we were fairly close, we rigged an aluminum ladder from the hatch down into the glider's cockpit, and I climbed down. That to me was the scariest part. In the cold weather my hands were numb, and going down that aluminum ladder I was wondering if there was any chance of the glider busting loose while I was getting into it. When I was all set I had them bring up the speed to forty knots [74 kph/46 mph]. We were headed into the wind towards the approach end of the field because I intended to circle it on the way down. The

Above : The worried pilot of a Curtiss XF9C-1 Sparrowhawk naval fighter looks anxiously upwards after hooking his aircraft onto the trapeze of the airship USS *Akron*. Designed specifically for airship duties, the Sparrowhawk occupies an almost unique position in aviation history as in its F9C-2 production form the only aircraft to be based on an airship.

captain started a countdown. He started with ten and at zero he cut her loose. I dropped like a flash. I wanted to be sure and get away from the airship because there were two big propellers ahead of me and three behind me. I wanted to get down quick, I levelled off about 50 feet [15 m]. From then on down it was duck soup. The only thing I was thinking of on the way down was a cup of hot coffee.'

Moffett's idea came to nothing, but *Akron* was duly completed, all 239 m (785 ft) of her. With her sister ship *Macon* she was the last of the great American rigid airships, and the fastest at 140 kph (87 mph). The Curtiss Aeroplane and Motor Company built six special F9C-2 Sparrowhawk hook-on fighters for the airships, to meet the US Navy's requirement for an aircraft which might easily pass through the 9.14-m by 7.32-m (30-ft by 24-ft) hangar opening beneath their hulls. The F9C-2 spanned 7.62 m (25 ft), had a 438-hp Wright engine and was armed with two 7.62-mm (0.3-in) machine-guns. *Akron* received her complement of aircraft in June 1932, ten months after she was commissioned, and tests soon realized her potential as an aircraft-carrier whose fighters could patrol beyond the horizon, controlled by radio from an airborne command post aboard the airship.

The Sparrowhawk pilots were truly 'daring young men on the flying trapeze', but both their dashing aerial ballet and the rigid airship were short-lived. *Akron* went down in the Atlantic on 3 April 1933 during a violent storm; 73 men died aboard her, including Admiral Moffett. The parasite experiments continued with *Macon* in an effort to justify her very existence to an increasingly sceptical Navy Board until 12 February 1935, when her top fin disintegrated in flight, half her helium escaped and like her sister

ship, *Macon* went into the sea, this time fortunately with the loss of only two lives. The US Navy's love affair with airships and trapeze aircraft was finished.

Pick-a-back fighters

Russia meanwhile was faced with much the same problem as America : far-flung borders to patrol with fighter aircraft of limited range. The ubiquitous Tupoler ANT-6, better known as the TB-3 bomber, provided an answer, though not the right one as it transpired. Experiments were conducted with fighter aircraft borne aloft on the fuselage and wings of TB-3s. They started modestly with two fighters, and slowly worked up to five, four of which were rolled up ramps on to cradles fixed to the bomber's wings, while a fifth joined up in flight, hooking on to yet another version of the trapeze gear used in British and American experiments. To help get this heavy formation airborne the engines of the wing-mounted fighters were run up at take-off; once up, the TB-3 could just maintain altitude under its own power.

The simultaneous departure of all five parasites from the mother ship in flight must have been an extraordinary sight, as was the composite creation of Imperial Airways' technical manager Major R. H. Mayo. Seeking an aircraft capable of flying the Atlantic with a sensible commercial payload, Mayo turned to advantage the ability of aircraft to carry a greater weight than they can lift from the ground. What if another aircraft were used to assist take-off, he wondered ? Taking as the basis for the mother ship an 'Empire' class flying-boat, Short Brothers adapted it as a carrier with a special superstructure for the smaller aircraft which would make the Atlantic crossing.

The converted 'Empire' boat was named *Maia* (Great One); above her sat *Mercury*, a purpose-built four-engined seaplane of exceptionally clean design.

This eight-engined part-time biplane composite was first tested on 4 January 1938. During take-off and before separation *Mercury*'s flying controls were automatically locked in the neutral position, *Maia*'s pilot having full command; the parasite's engines were started from inside the mother ship and combined with those of *Maia* to get the two components airborne. The first separation was made with complete success over Rochester, Kent one month after the maiden composite flight, and preparations began for a transatlantic proving flight, which was to be the first commercial crossing with a payload by a heavier-than-air craft. At 7.58 p.m. on 20 July 1938 *Mercury* parted company with *Maia* over Foynes Harbour, County Limerick, Ireland crewed by Captain Donald Bennett (later of Pathfinder fame) and radio operator A. J. Coster. *Mercury* carried 5455 litres (1200 Imperial gallons) of fuel in its wings and 508 kg (1120 lb) of newspapers, mail and newsreel footage in her twin floats, including film of the arrival in Dublin two days previously of American airman Doug 'Wrong Way' Corrigan, who crossed the Atlantic after leaving New York allegedly bound for California, and having misread his compass he claimed.

Instead of refuelling at Newfoundland, Bennett flew on to Montreal nonstop, covering the 4715 km (2930 miles) from Ireland in 13 hours 29 minutes, then set off again for New York, where for the first time ever English newspapers were on sale at the news-stands on the day after publication, thanks to Mayo's pick-a-back aircraft. In October 1938 *Mercury* and Bennett made news again with a nonstop flight of 9728 km (6045 miles) from Dundee, Scotland to Orange River, South Africa in 42 hours 5 minutes. The Composite subsequently operated a scheduled nonstop mail service between Southampton and Alexandria, Egypt which continued until the outbreak of World War II.

Deadly mistletoe
Composite aircraft enabled packages more deadly than mail to be delivered during World War II, when the German Junkers company and DFS (*Deutsches Forschungsinstitut für Segelflug*) developed the *Mistel* (Mistletoe), which comprised an unmanned bomber packed with explosive and a pick-a-back fighter whose pilot would fly the missile to its target.

Tests began in 1942, using a DFS 230 glider as the lower component, with Klemm and Focke-Wulf lightplanes as carriers. For full-scale trials a Junkers Ju 88A-4 bomber was selected as the missile, fitted with an armour-piercing warhead containing 1725 kg (3803 lb) of impact-fused high explosive. The mother ship (the Germans called it *Vater* or *Father*; Freud would have understood, no doubt) was a Messerschmitt Bf 109F-4. In normal flight a three-axis autopilot steered the combination on command from the fighter pilot whose control inputs were made on two thumb-buttons (rudder and aileron were linked), but for coarse control inputs or large course corrections the Bf 109F's control column and rudder pedals could be used to operate the surfaces of both aircraft. The fighter separated from the bomber over the target by means of mechanical or explosive links. A number of different *Mistel* composites were developed, using Junkers Ju 88s and various marks of Messerschmitt Bf 109 and Focke-Wulf Fw 190, and others were planned which were to have used Messerschmitt Me 262, Arado Ar 234 and Heinkel He 162 jets as the upper components.

The first operational use of *Misteln* was to have been an attack on the Royal Navy anchorage at Scapa Flow from an airfield on the coast of Denmark, but the Allied invasion of Normandy on 6 June 1944 brought a hasty transference of 2./KG 101's *Mistel* 1s (Ju 88A-4/Bf 109F-4) to St Dizier, whence

Below : The Short Composite was developed during the 1930s in an attempt to provide fast mailplanes with an aerial boost by lifting them into the air on top of a larger aircraft, then releasing them to make a heavily-laden dash at high speed with the payload. Conceived by Major R. H. Mayo of Imperial Airways, the idea was exhaustively tested and proved successful by the Composite: the mother ship was a modified Short 'Empire' class flying-boat, while the mailplane was a specially designed high-speed mailplane, named *Mercury*.

five *Mistel* composites attacked invasion shipping on the night of 24 June (all *Misteln* were operated under cover of darkness because of their lack of defensive armament). Four successful hits were claimed, the fifth Ju 88 having to be jettisoned. Some 82 *Misteln* were ready for operation by March 1945, and were employed primarily in bridge attacks (the warhead was capable of penetrating up to 18 m/60 ft of concrete), their final sortie taking place on 16 April against Soviet bridgeheads.

Aerial parasites
Like their namesakes, parasite aircraft are hard to keep at bay. When the gargantuan Convair B-36 Peacemaker bomber went into service with the United States Air Force's Strategic Air Command, plans were laid for two hook-on projects.

The first of these was a tiny, ugly aluminium bug of a fighter called the McDonnell XF-85 Goblin, which was barely 4.57 m (15 ft) long and had the appearance of a jet-propelled bumble bee. The stubby little Goblin was to have been carried in the B-36's bomb-bay ready for launching in the event of fighter attack. Having won the ensuing dogfight it would then rejoin the mother ship; it had to, for McDonnell did not give it any landing gear of its own.

The first of two Goblins flew on 23 August 1948, but hook-up tests on a Boeing B-29 Superfortress revealed a fatal flaw which had earlier been encountered (though to a lesser degree) with the airship carriers in the 1930s: severe turbulence near the bomber made it all but impossible to hook-on, and on one occasion the trapeze smashed through the Goblin's cockpit canopy. Difficulties with the aircraft and the development of long-range jet bombers brought the programme to a halt.

The second attempt to use the B-36 as an aircraft-carrier took place in 1955 and 1956. Seeking a reconnaissance aircraft with sufficient range to reach the Soviet Union, the USAF came up with FICON, which stood for Fighter In CONvair. By hitching a Republic RF-84 Thunderflash to a B-36, the photo-reconnaissance jet's range could be extended from 3220 km (2000 miles) to 19,310 km (12,000 miles). Some thought was also given to a nuclear-bomb equipped Thunderstreak substituting for the Thunderflash when SAC wanted to hit with something harder than cameras. Twenty-five RF-84FS were modified for parasite duty. On a typical mission the mother ship B-36 would depart from Fairchild Air Force Base, Spokane, Washington to be joined in the air by an RF-84K (as the parasite Thunderflashes were designated) from Moses Lake Air Force Base, 160 km (100 miles) away. The fighter would be hoisted into the B-36's bomb bay,

Left : A factory photograph reveals the squat proportions of the tiny McDonnell XF-85 Goblin parasite fighter. The retractable trapeze was to be installed in B-36 bombers, allowing Goblins to operate from them as escort fighters at very long range, the retractable hook on the nose of the XF-85 allowing the aircraft to be deployed and then recovered.

Below : Air launches from a mother ship are of great use in test programmes, allowing the experimental aircraft to be freed of the weight and complexity of an under-carriage. Such an aircraft was the rocket-powered Bell X-1A.

with wings and tail sticking out, and the pilot could climb aboard the bomber and ride in comfort to his mission site.

There is a story that a young, naive duty officer at Moses Lake once refused an RF-84K pilot clearance for a 16-hour mission for which no stops or refuellings were listed because the flight was apparently way beyond the aircraft's endurance. He had never been told about the FICON, apparently.

Most of the flying lift-thumbers we have looked at so far have had one primary purpose: increased range. Air-to-air refuelling techniques have made parasite aircraft and composites redundant for long-distance flying, but there is still an application for pick-a-back aircraft for which no substitute has been found: research.

On 14 October 1947 the Bell X-1 rocket research aircraft was carried aloft beneath a Boeing B-29 mother ship with Captain Charles E. 'Chuck' Yeager at the controls. In Yeager's own words:

'Prior to the drop you always had a feeling of anticipation. You wondered whether or not everything would work out all right . . . Once you were dropped, at about 25,000 feet [7620 m], you were on your own and you felt perfectly at home. Actually, you just sort of floated a little bit when the mechanism released you from the B-29. You were subject to a falling sensation for a minute until you could level the airplane out and fire your rockets, and then it flew like a conventional airplane, except that you had rocket power and no noise and no moving parts. I've tried to think back to that first flight past Mach One, but it doesn't seem any more important than the others. I was at about 37,000 feet [11,280 m] straight level, and it was just a matter of flying the airplane. It flew very nicely and got up to .97 on the Mach indicator, and then the meter jumped to about 1.05 as I accelerated past the shock wave that was on the nose of the airplane. I was kind of disappointed that it wasn't more of a big charge than it was.'

This was man's first level-flight super-sonic trip, thanks to a lift from the Super-fortress mother ship. The Bell X-1 and X-2 programmes relied on air-launches, as did the North American X-15 which was carried beneath a Boeing B-52 Stratofortress jet bomber and flew faster and higher than any other manned aircraft, reaching a maximum speed of Mach 6.72 and an altitude of 108 km (67 miles).

Hitching a ride into space

But the ultimate pick-a-back aircraft is surely NASA's Space Shuttle, the world's heaviest, most expensive glider, which has been test-launched from the back of a modi-fied Boeing 747 airliner and will inaugurate a new era of American space exploration for the 1980s, riding up into orbit on the back of a pair of solid rocket boosters each providing 1,315,430-kg (2,900,000-lb) thrust.

Chapter 13

THE BIG THE SMALL & THE UGLY

Special requirements have frequently led to special aircraft, and these have often been notable for various physical extremes: the Convair B-36 strategic bomber was an enormous aircraft powered by six piston engines and four jet engines; the Stits Sky Baby, on the other hand, was designed merely to be the world's smallest aircraft; and the extraordinary McDonnell XF-85 Goblin had the most unusual appearance to suit it for parasite operations.

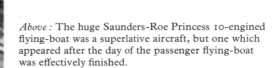

Above: The huge Saunders-Roe Princess 10-engined flying-boat was a superlative aircraft, but one which appeared after the day of the passenger flying-boat was effectively finished.

Left: Perhaps one of the ugliest, but most useful, aircraft of its period, the Aero Spacelines Super Guppy is designed for the carriage of outsize cargoes such as whole missiles or aircraft components.

VISITORS TO THE biennial aviation bazaar at the Paris Air Show in the 1960s and early 1970s were witness to an amusing game of cold-war one-upmanship between the Soviet Union and United States. At every Salon there would be a tantalizing gap in the list of Russian exhibits for an 'unspecified aircraft type', and rumours abounded as to what spectacular aircraft they might come up with each time. In 1971 the Americans presented their immense Lockheed C-5A Galaxy military transport in a confident 'top that if you can' gesture. The Russians did; they brought their gigantic Mil V-12 helicopter, whose twin rotors span just 1 m (3 ft) less than the C-5A's wings.

Coincidentally, the world's first very large aircraft was Russian. In 1912 Igor Sikorsky began construction of an aircraft which was revolutionary in several ways: with a wingspan of 28 m (92 ft) it was at that time by far the largest heavier-than-air craft to fly; the first to have four engines; the first with a fully-enclosed passenger cabin; and the first designed specifically as an airliner.

Officially known as *Russkii Vitiaz* (Russian Knight), the big biplane was dubbed the *Grand* or *Bolshoi* before its first flight on 13 May 1913. The *Grand* weighed 4080 kg (9000 lb) and was powered by four 100-hp water-cooled Argus engines arranged initially in tandem pairs to mitigate the effects of asymmetric thrust in the event of engine failure, but after the first ten-minute test flight the two rear-mounted engines were moved outboard on the wings.

Numerous difficulties were encountered in the design and construction of so large an aircraft just ten years after the Wright Brothers' first flight. Sikorsky's colleagues warned him that the machine was simply too big and too heavy to rise from the ground, and too cumbersome to be controlled if it did manage to fly. Most importantly, they pointed to the danger of trying to pilot an aircraft from an enclosed cabin with no wind on the cheek from which to judge attitude. Other problems were more basic; there were no wheels of adequate size to support the *Grand*, so a 16-wheel bogie undercarriage had to be built, just like those used on heavy transport jets today. The cabin incorporated some novelties. At the front was a large open balcony with a searchlight mounted on a gimbal; next came the cockpit with dual controls for two pilots; behind this was the passenger cabin, luxuriously appointed with four seats, sofa, table, washroom and ward-

Built by the Russo-Baltic Wagon Works to a design by Sikorsky, the *Grand* was a world-leader in its day, opening up the prospect if not the reality of passenger transport in giant aircraft.

robe. 'It was', said Sikorsky, 'like something out of Jules Verne though not so impractical.'

On its first flight from St Petersburg Sikorsky took along on the *Grand*'s front balcony a mechanic whose job it was to move back and forth through the cabin to trim the craft should it prove nose or tail heavy. In the event he was able to remain at his station, waving to the crowds below as the heavy biplane lumbered laboriously up to 240 m (800 ft). The *Grand* flew well, however, and subsequently made 53 flights including a record-breaking duration flight of 1 hour 53 minutes with eight people aboard on 2 August 1913. Later that month a military Voisin biplane broke up in the air over the airfield and its engine fell onto the *Grand*.

Sikorsky subsequently redesigned the aircraft as the *Ilya Muromets* which was even bigger; on 11 February 1914 this machine set a new world record by carrying aloft 16 people and a dog. A familiar picture of it shows the big biplane landing with two fur-coated passengers taking a stroll along its fuselage-top promenade.

The *Ilya Muromets* went into production as a heavy bomber for the Imperial Russian Air Service. Seventy-three were built, and they were so effective on more than 400 bombing raids against Germany and Lithuania in 1915 that Great Britain and France sought permission from Czar Nicholas II to produce the design under licence, though nothing came of the scheme before the 1917 Russian Revolution sent Sikorsky fleeing to the United States.

Sikorsky established a precedent among Soviet designers for large aircraft. Andrei Nikolaevich Tupolev, who helped establish Russia's Central Aerohydrodynamic Institute after the revolution, and subsequently headed its design department, caught the giant plane bug in 1929. He designed the ANT-14, a five-engined airliner powered by Soviet-built Bristol Jupiter radial engines: this spanned 40 m (132 ft) and could carry 42 people over the then not inconsiderable distance of 1200 km (745 miles), sufficient to fly in stages from Moscow to Vladivostock. The ANT-14 was modestly successful, serving on the Moscow-Berlin route and on scientific explorations in Siberia and the Arctic, but Tupolev wanted to build an even bigger machine, the ANT-16, which was a six-engined behemoth of such poor performance that the Soviet government declined further support for Tupolev's large aircraft.

Unshaken by this official lack of confidence, Tupolev began planning his *magnum opus* – the world's largest aircraft – and found support in the unlikely shape of the Union of Soviet Writers and Publishers who were seeking a spectacular celebration for the 40th anniversary of writer Maxim Gorki's literary debut. Workers all over Russia donated money for the construction of not just one giant aircraft, but a whole *Maxim Gorki Propaganda Squadron* of them, for which 6,000,000 roubles were collected.

When it appeared at Moscow's Central Airport in the spring of 1934, Tupolev's first ANT-20 *Maxim Gorki* was indeed a gargantuan tribute to its author namesake, spanning 63 m (206 ft), which is more than the span of a Boeing 747, with eight engines totalling 7200 hp, and a gross weight of 52.8 tonnes (52 tons). Its wheelpants were as big

Right: Derived from the *Grand*, the Sikorsky *Ilya Muromets* turned the concept of four-engined aircraft into a practical reality. Note the two intrepid passengers taking a walk on the promenade deck above the rear fuselage. A useful load-lifter, the *Ilya Muromets* was developed into a heavy bomber during World War I.

as buses, and within its fuselage and cavernous wings were seats for up to 80 passengers, a cinema, newspaper office, darkroom, printing press, radio station, buffet bar, toilets, sleeping quarters and an internal telephone exchange. Beneath its wings loudspeakers and illuminated signs were installed to broadcast political slogans; engineers could walk through the inside of the structure to attend to its engines.

Giant disaster

This aerial *tour de force* flew for the first time on 19 May 1934. One year later workers at the institute were invited to fly in the giant machine which they had designed and built. Thirty-six passengers boarded, along with 11 crew, and *Maxim Gorki* took off, accompanied by a fighter which was to formate with it for air-to-air photographs. During the flight the fighter pilot, named Blagin, took it upon himself to do some unauthorized aerobatics, became disorientated during a barrel roll and collided with the *Gorki*, which broke up in the air and exploded in a massive fireball, throwing bodies and equipment out in full view of spectators at the airport. All 47 aboard the giant aircraft died, together with Blagin (whose name subsequently was vilified in Russia) and three bystanders. Interestingly, the accident evoked the same response outside Russia as major air crashes do today: that aircraft were getting too big for their own good. The Russians evidently disagreed, for they immediately subscribed for three more ANT-20s, with just six engines of greater power, and eventually 16 were built, eight of which survived World War II.

Before the appearance of Tupolev's mon-

strosities, Germany held claim to the world's largest aircraft. In 1926 Claude Dornier, a protégé of Count von Zeppelin, began design work on a transatlantic flying boat which would carry 100 passengers. The Dornier Do X ('X' for unknown quantity) weighed 62 tonnes (61 tons) loaded, spanned 48 m (157 ft), had three decks, and was powered by 12 Siemens-built Bristol Jupiter radial engines mounted in tandem pairs atop a forest of struts above its great plank-like wing.

The Do X began flying off the Bodensee on 25 July 1929. In October of that year it took off with the greatest number of people to date carried by one aircraft: 169, made up of ten crew, 150 passengers and nine stowaways. Dornier's former employer, von Zeppelin, was dismayed: his airships, based just across the lake from where the Do X flew, could carry less than half that number.

But the Dornier was a dismal performer, barely able to climb above 400 m (1312 ft) because of the poor cooling of the rear-mounted sextet of Jupiters, which sharply reduced their power output. A dozen liquid-cooled Curtiss Conqueror engines of 600 hp each were substituted, and the big boat's ceiling went up, but only to 490 m (1610 ft).

On 2 November 1930 the Do X set off from Friedrichshafen on a transatlantic proving and publicity flight in the hands of Captain Friedrich Christiansen, journeying via Amsterdam and Calshot to Lisbon, where a fire broke out in the wing, delaying the trip for a month. Taking off from Las Palmas in the Canary Islands in high seas the hull took such a beating that another three months were wasted for repairs.

Above : A monster by the standards of any time, the Dornier Do X flying-boat was at first powered by 12 licence-built Bristol Jupiter radial engines (seen here). With these engines performance was poor, and so 12 Curtiss Conqueror inlines were substituted, with little effect on performance. The real trouble lay in the fact that the Do X was too heavy and had too small a wing area.

Eventually the 12-engined titan reached Natal, Brazil after crossing the Atlantic at an altitude of 6 m (20 ft) and with half her crew of 19 and much of her cargo of mail left behind to save weight. The new engines, while giving more power than the radials, burned fuel at the astonishing rate of 1820 litres (400 Imperial gallons) per hour, which meant that every non-essential item had to be sacrificed to quench the Conquerors' thirst. At length, on 27 August 1931, the Do X came roaring across New York's Battery to a ticker-tape welcome, ten months after setting out from Germany on a desultory trip whose average speed had been less than 3 kph (2 mph). Two further Do Xs were built for the Italian air force, while the inefficient but magnificent prototype ended its days in the *Deutsches Luftfahrt Museum* (German Air Transport Museum) in Berlin, where an Allied bomb destroyed it during World War II.

While Dornier was working on his elephantine flying-boat, Professor Hugo Junkers was designing a large bat-winged airliner, culminating 20 years of research on flying-wing transports. As early as 1909 Junkers had been projecting aircraft capable of carrying as many as 1000 people (something no aircraft has yet done). Recognizing, however, that his flying wings were over-ambitious, he started work in 1928 on a machine which incorporated much of his flying-wing technology, but had a conventional fuselage and empennage.

A tailed flying wing

The Junkers G-38's 44-m (144-ft) wing was 1.7 m (5 ft 7 in) thick at the root, enabling four passengers to be housed there, looking out through glazed leading edges, while the other 30 travellers sat in the fuselage. The thick wing also gave inflight access to the four engines, initially two each of 400 hp and 800 hp, but later changed to 800-hp Junkers L.88s, and finally to Jumo 204 diesel engines which left characteristic black trails like modern jets using water-injection.

Two G-38s, named *Deutschland* and *Generalfeldmarschall von Hindenburg*, went into service with Deutsche Lufthansa in 1930 and 1931 on the important routes from Berlin to Copenhagen, Venice and Rome, bringing with them new standards of passenger comfort with two-deck accommodation, smoking rooms and washrooms. One crashed in 1936; the second example was destroyed in a bombing raid.

During World War II Junkers employed a wing like that of the G-38 on a massive transport glider design, the Ju 322 *Mammut* (Mammoth) which was abandoned in favour of the Messerschmitt Me 321 *Gigant* (Giant) when stability problems showed up on its first test flight. The 62-m (203-ft) span glider

Right : The Junkers G-38 was one of the largest aircraft of its time, and came relatively close to achieving Professor Junkers's concept of a passenger-carrying flying-wing. It was in fact little more than a flying-wing with small stabilizing surfaces at the end of a short fuselage.

Below: With Howard Hughes at the controls, the huge Hercules flying-boat makes its one flight. Flown on 2 November 1947 this covered about 1.6 km (1 mile) at about 160 kph (100 mph). The Hercules, having vindicated its designer, was then returned to its hangar, where it has been maintained ever since with the aid of finance set aside by its eccentric designer.

reared above the Junkers Ju 90 towplane (for whose take-off 5 km (3 miles) of forest had been cleared from the end of the Junkers airfield at Mersburg) and had to be cast off, landing in a meadow where it lay for two weeks before it was towed back to the airfield by the two tanks it had been designed to carry. Both it and 99 other *Mammuts* under construction were sawn up into neat blocks for firewood.

The *Gigant* might well have been better off had the same early fate befallen it. Designed to meet the transport requirement which had spawned the Junkers machine, the Messerschmitt Me 321 was only slightly smaller at 55 m (180 ft), and was intended to ferry into combat 22.5 tonnes (22 tons) of equipment or a company of soldiers complete with 88-mm flak gun or tracked vehicle. The Me 321 had to be towed up by a formation of three Messerschmitt Bf 110 twin-engined fighters, or four Junkers Ju 52/3m tri-motor transports, or the extraordinary Heinkel He 111 *Zwilling* (Twin). The last consisted of two Heinkel He 111 twin-engined medium bombers joined together by an extra wing section carrying a fifth engine. Early trials of the *Gigant* glider were conducted with rocket-assisted take-off. On one occasion the rockets on one side of the aircraft failed, slewing it wildly and dragging its three tow planes together, and the whole formation crashed killing the 120 troops aboard the *Gigant*, its crew of six and the three Bf 110 pilots. At the time it was the world's worst air crash, though the Germans never claimed the dubious record. The diminutive Hanna Reitsch, who flew the *Gigant* once (and only once), said of it: 'Impossible . . . It was so difficult to fly; you needed so much strength, and what was too hard for me on a five-minute flight would be too much for a strong man on a one-hour flight.'

Despite her warnings to Ernst Udet and to Willi Messerschmitt, the *Gigant* went into production, as did a six-engine powered version, the Me 323, which was slow, plagued with engine overheating problems and was as hated by the German troops who had to ride in it (they called Me 323s 'sticking plaster bombers') as it was loved by Allied fighter pilots who found the lumbering, inflammable giant an easy target.

'Spruce Goose'

The need to transport large numbers of troops and tons of equipment in wartime also inspired another giant on the other side of the Atlantic. Howard Hughes, oil-drilling equipment billionaire, movie-mogul and record-breaking aviator designed a flying-boat which would ferry supplies across the sea to Europe free from the U-boat threat. Hughes's conception was not just any fly-

ing-boat, but one so immense, so staggering in concept that it seemed like a hoax. His aircraft's stabilizer was to be 3.05 m (10 ft) bigger than the wing of a Boeing B-17 Flying Fortress bomber; its own wing would span 97.5 m (320 ft), and it would be capable of carrying 700 men. Most improbably of all, it would be constructed from wood.

The design problems which Hughes and his team encountered in creating a 183-tonne (180-ton) aircraft from non-strategic materials delayed the project until after the war, when there was no longer any pressing need for such a machine, when Hughes, smarting from criticism over the $40,000,000 tax dollars expended on the flying-boat, determined to finish it at his own expense. So big was the Hercules, known colloquially as 'the flying lumber yard', 'the flying coffin' or simply (and most commonly) 'Spruce Goose', that a firm of house movers had to be engaged to transport its 66.75-m (219-m) laminated plywood hull along specially laid roads from Culver City, California to Terminal Island, Long Beach where final assembly began in June 1946.

'It will never fly' was the most commonly expressed sentiment on the Long Beach waterfront for the next 18 months (and by the government, which attempted to retrieve its funding on the grounds that the Spruce Goose was unflyable). On 2 November 1947 Hughes, familiar trilby hat in place, boarded the Hercules, started the eight 3000-hp Pratt & Whitney Wasp Major engines and taxied out into the bay, ostensibly for water-handling tests. Once on the open water, however, Hughes opened up the Spruce Goose's 24,000 hp and took off, flying for about 0.6 km (1 mile) at a height of 6 m (20 ft). The Hercules never flew again. It was stored in a specially constructed hangar at Long Beach, where it remains today, heavily guarded by Hughes employees, the largest aircraft ever to fly. Some say that having proved his point that the machine could fly, Hughes simply lost interest; others claim that even in those few brief moments of flight the Hercules creaked and groaned and handled so badly that Hughes never dared fly it again. One thing is certain, though: Howard Hughes was the only man ever to fly in the largest flying machine yet made by man unless, as it is rumoured, a stowaway really did sneak aboard.

Coincident with Hughes's ideas for the Hercules in 1941, the United States Army Air Force began planning an intercontinental-range strategic bomber capable of striking at Nazi-held Europe from American bases and returning after delivering a 4535-kg (10,000-lb) bomb load. Consolidated Aircraft (later Convair) won the contract for a prototype, designated XB-36, but the project languished when events in Europe took

a turn for the better for the Allies, and the first aircraft was not completed until September 1945.

The XB-36 was a most unconventional aircraft. With an enormous 70-m (230-ft) wing and six engines of over 3000-hp each driving pusher propellers, it weighed 102 tonnes (100 tons) and excepting the grounded Hercules it became another 'world's largest'. The tyres on its main landing gear were 2.74 m (9 ft) in diameter (they also concentrated too much weight on the runways of the day, and were replaced on production aircraft by four-wheel bogie units), and the pressurized fore-and-aft crew areas at each end of its massive bomb bay were linked by a 24.4-m (80-ft) tunnel through which crewmen rode on a wheeled trolley.

Later production models of the B-36 'Thundering Peacemaker' had four 2360-kg (5200-lb) thrust J47 jet engines in underslung pods to boost performance; with the six piston engines also uprated to 3800 hp each, the B-36 was the world's most powerful aircraft, as well as its largest.

In its final production version the B-36J had a combat overload weight of 208 tonnes (205 tons), more than double that of the prototype, and a maximum flight duration of 42 hours. An arsenal of 16 guns was carried, and crews numbered between 13 and 22 men, depending on the model and type of mission, some of which involved high-altitude overflights of the Soviet Union. The Thundering Peacemaker was also the mother ship for parasite aircraft operations (*see Chapter 12*) using Republic RF-84K Thunderflash photo-reconnaissance fighters slung beneath its belly. In its heyday the B-36 reigned supreme, flying at altitudes close to 18,290 m (60,000 ft), where few other aircraft could operate effectively. The type was one which crews either loved or hated. 'That was a horrible, lazy beast to fly,' says one former B-36 man. 'If I had to fly it again, I think I'd join the infantry.'

Too big and too late

The British also had a brief and inglorious flirtation with giant aircraft after World War II. Both projects were airliners, the first devised by a committee (as such madnesses often are) headed by Lord Brabazon of Tara, an aristocratic aviation pioneer who once proved right the old adage that 'pigs might fly' by giving one a ride in his Voisin biplane. This airliner was supposed to be able to carry 100 passengers nonstop from London to New York in ocean liner luxury, and when the Bristol Aeroplane Company was given leave to proceed with two prototypes the name Brabazon was chosen for the type.

Six and a half years later, in 1949, the first Brabazon was ready at Filton near Bristol,

Above: The huge Convair B-36 strategic bomber of the late 1940s was powered by six massive radials engines driving pusher propellers; but even these gave the aircraft a lumbering performance only, and matters were improved finally by the addition of four jet engines in two pods under the outer wing panels.

Right : The Bristol Brabazon was a misconceived but important effort by the British to regain a foothold in the long-range airliner business after World War II, and was powered by eight radial piston engines geared in pairs to power four large tractor propellers.

where an entire village had been flattened to provide a 2515-m (8250-ft) runway for the monster, which was longer than Convair's B-36, but identical in span and stood 15.25 m (50 ft) high to the tip of its Union Jack-bedecked fin. Eight 2500-hp Bristol Centaurus piston engines driving contra-rotating propellers were mounted in pairs within its fat wing. The maiden flight took place on 4 September 1949 before a crowd of pressmen and VIPs. Test pilot Bill Pegg recalls:

'My first impression was one of tremendous size. Of course, it was a big aeroplane, but these things should be comparative, and I had never had quite this feeling of vastness, even stepping out of a Spitfire to fly a Lancaster. I was sitting in the cockpit and looking out of windscreens not much larger than before, and felt that this end seemed to be operating pretty well, but what about the rest of it coming along behind! I remember thinking about this and my mind goes back to the first time I heard the question: "Oh, Mr. Pegg, what is it really like to fly such a gigantic aeroplane?" My answer was, "It's quite easy, we just fly the cockpit and the rest of it trails along." '

On that first flight the rest of it' trailed along nicely and the test flights went so well that the Brabazon was flown to the Farnborough Air Show with only three hours' total flying time, before touring seaside resorts to give taxpayers a sight of the aircraft their money had paid for (Concorde, which was also built at Filton, made a similar propaganda tour, though it cost forty times per head of population what the Brabazon had). Everyone, including the author who was four years old at the time, was impressed, but already the aircraft was as good as dead. It had been conceived in 1943, when runways around the world were short. Its thick wing was designed to lift its immense weight at low airspeeds (160 kph/100 mph at take-off, which used less than half the extended Filton runway, much to the chagrin of villagers who had lost their homes), but was hopelessly inefficient for high-speed flight. The Brabazon was too slow, and American airliners then reaching the market offered better performance at much lower cost. Late in 1952 the British government reported that 'neither the civil airlines nor fighting services could foresee any economic use for it' and ordered the prototype, with 400 hours of flight time, and a second unfinished Brabazon to be broken up. It was a scrap dealer's bonanza, for the two machines and all the jigs were sold for a paltry £10,000, though they cost £12,500,000. Today all that remains of this disastrous 'committee' aircraft is a giant wheel on show at the Science Museum in London.

The second of these follies was a leviathan of a flying-boat called the Saunders-Roe Princess, 10.2 tonnes (10 tons) heavier than

the Brabazon and intended as a flagship for British Overseas Airways Corporation. This time the idea came from the post-war Labour government in Britain who were more convinced than the airline itself that BOAC needed the aircraft.

The name Princess (originally it had been planned to call the aircraft Dollar Princess, since its prime purpose was to earn money from rich Americans on transatlantic routes) was singularly inappropriate for a corpulent whale of an aircraft which weighed 152 tonnes (150 tons) and was to have carried 105 passengers in its two-deck, pressurized hull. The Princess was 30.5 m (100 ft) shorter in span than the Spruce Goose, powered by ten Bristol Proteus turboprop engines, eight of them coupled in pairs driving contra-rotating propellers. Like the Hughes boat

Above: Despite the failure of their Princess flying-boat, Saunders-Roe in the late 1940s urged the development of an even larger flying-boat, with four decks and powered by no less than 24 turbojets buried in the wings.

Right: No greater contrast in sizes can be found than by comparing the gigantic Princess derivative above with the diminutive Stits Junior.

and the Brabazon, the Princess devoured money. By the time the first example flew, years behind schedule, in August 1952 the programme cost had nearly quadrupled to £11,000,000 and the only people to have made a profit on the giant flying-boat were the owners of pleasure launches who could barely keep pace with the demand from sightseers wanting to ride out into the Solent where flight testing was being conducted.

Meanwhile the customer, BOAC, had given up flying-boat operations. No-one wanted the orphan Princess or her two sisterships which had been completed at Saunders-Roe's Isle of Wight factory, and once again the government called a halt. The three Princesses, last vestiges of Britain's glorious flying-boat history, sat cocooned at Calshot, former base of the Schneider Trophy-winning RAF High Speed Flight, for 15 years before the cutters' torches finally destroyed them. Grand schemes to re-engine them with nuclear powerplants in place of the troubled coupled Proteuses came to nothing, and Saunders-Roe's plans for a 681-tonne (670-ton) 'Jet Princess' powered by 24 Rolls-Royce Conway engines and carrying 1000 passengers never was more than a glimmer of hope killed off by the flood of land-based jet airliners which ended for all time the commercial flying-boat era.

A mite amongst leviathans

To end this parade of giants, and to give it some scale, there is the Stits Sky Baby, the world's smallest aircraft. This is so tiny that 45 of them could have fitted wingtip-to-wingtip along the Spruce Goose's wing. The Sky Baby was fathered by an American designer and homebuilder named Ray Stits, who built his first small plane in 1948. That was called the Junior and spanned 2.7 m (8 ft 10 in). No sooner had Stits completed it than word spread that someone was working on a design just a fraction smaller. Not about to be inched out of his record, Stits set to work again and finished the Sky Baby at his Riverside, California workshop in the summer of 1952. It was incredibly small, with biplane wings just 2.18 m (7 ft 2 in) in span; a long-armed pilot could sit in the cockpit and reach out to the tip of each coffee-table sized wing.

The Sky Baby was powered by a 112-hp Continental engine, race-tuned, which gave it a maximum speed close to 322 kph (200 mph). Only one man ever flew it – Bob Starr, Ray Stits' partner, who had the experience and outstanding piloting qualities which the tricky midget apparently demanded. The Sky Baby still holds the title of world's smallest aircraft, and is likely to for ever. It is preserved at the Experimental Aircraft Association's museum in a suburb of Milwaukee, Wisconsin.

Chapter 14
PEDAL PLANES

The lure of man-powered flight has always been a strong one, rooted in the very concept of the birdman syndrome. Despite its apparent simplicity, however, man-powered flight is extremely difficult, men's muscles not being designed for such high-power, high-endurance activities. Many men tried and failed, others tried and partially succeeded, and then in less than two years pilot Bryan Allen scooped the two most important man-powered prizes in the beautifully conceived and executed Gossamer Condor and Gossamer Albatross, flying a large figure 8 in the former, and the English Channel in the latter.

Above: The Stark man-powered flyabout was patented in 1893 by one Theodore Stark, and was intended as a sport aircraft. Power was to be taken from the prone pilot's hands and feet by an endless belt. Needless to say, it could not and did not fly.

Left: The spidery grace of the Gossamer Condor is well shown.

I N FRENCH IT is called *vol musculaire*, a phrase which describes perfectly the panting, perspiring, puffing world of man-powered flight.

Flight powered solely by human muscle|is nothing new, of course; many of the early birdmen *(see Chapter 1)* thought that if birds could fly on muscle power, then so could men. They overlooked man's poor performance as an energy producer compared with birds, which have an enormous energy output for their body weight, while even a highly trained, super-fit athlete can only manage an output of half a horsepower for a sustained period. Little chance, then, that man would ever flap his way into the skies on strength of arm alone.

But if he combined muscle power with some kind of mechanical contrivance, what then? Leonardo da Vinci believed man-powered flight was possible. 'A bird is an instrument working according to mathematical law,' he wrote in his *Codex Atlanticus*, 'an instrument which is within the capacity of man to reproduce with all its movements, though not with a corresponding degree of strength ... We may therefore say that such an instrument constructed by man is lacking in nothing except the life of a bird, and this life must needs be supplied from that of man.' Da Vinci sketched a number of designs for ornithopters whose wings were flapped by pulleys and levers operated by foot stirrups; from his anatomical studies Leonardo knew that thigh and leg muscles were much more likely to provide the necessary power than the weaker chest muscles. Da Vinci was only a theorist, however, and never attempted to fly one of his machines.

Four centuries later an American professor of physics named Harry LaVerne Twining, whose previous noteworthy research included an attempt to weigh the souls of dead mice, reached much the same conclusion as Leonardo and built himself a man-powered ornithopter which was tested late in 1909. It consisted of a tricycle to which articulated 8.2-m (27-ft) wings, operated by foot stirrups, were attached. The *Los Angeles Daily Times* dubbed it 'Twining's Flip-Flop' and assured worried readers that Twining did not intend to rise far from the ground at first, which was just as well because the flip-flop was a complete flop, flapping furiously along a Los Angeles street but barely rising an inch. A British man-powered aircraft constructed that same year adopted a different approach, using a pedal-driven propeller for thrust and fixed wings for lift. This was the Druiff-Neate Cyclo-Aeroplane, of which little information survives save for a photograph which shows it to have had a tiny wing and an equally tiny, Chaplinesque inventor.

The man-powered flying movement was boosted in 1912 by French automobile manufacturers Peugeot, who launched a 10,000-franc competition for the first man to fly 10 m (32¾ ft) without a motor. One hundred and ninety-eight entrants registered for the contest, and in the months preceding the first trials winged bicycles were a not uncommon sight whizzing, earth-bound, along French lanes. On the appointed day, 2 June 1912, just 23 'Aviettes' appeared for the fly-off, by which time Peugeot, realizing that their original goal had been too ambitious, offered instead 1000 francs to anyone who could fly just 1 m (3¼ ft) at a height not less than 10 cm (4 in). There were some novel entries, including one from a *Monsieur* Didier, sporting a pair of butterfly wings on its handlebars; Count de Guiseux's Aeroplane Bicycle had boxkite-shaped 'wings' and a chain-driven propeller; and a cycle racer named Lavalade claimed during trials to have flown more than the specified distance, but only after pedalling off the end of an inclined ramp. Of Lavalade's effort *Flying* magazine reported that 'the wings seem more of a hindrance to getting up speed than a help when Lavalade makes his wheel hop.'

The Peugeot prize was not won until 9 July 1921 when Gabriel Poulain made two dawn flights on his 'aerocycle' at Longchamps racetrack, travelling about 10.6 m (35 ft) at a height of 1 m (3¼ ft). Peugeot immediately posted a 20,000-franc reward for a 50-m (164-ft) flight, but it was never claimed.

Enter the Germans

In view of the pioneering efforts of the birdman Otto Lilienthal, it was fitting that the first serious, scientific attempts at man-powered flight should have taken place in Germany. The Treaty of Versailles banned powered flying and thus in the years following the end of World War I great emphasis was placed on soaring, and, to a lesser extent, *Muskelflug*. Prominent among the experimenters, and first to achieve a measure of success, was Alexander Lippisch, later to become famous as the inventor of the delta wing *(see Chapter 5)*. In 1929 he built a flapping-wing glider on which the wing movement was operated by the pilot's legs in the manner of one of those rowing machine keep-fit devices. Lippisch's aircraft was launched by a rubber bungee, and was therefore man-assisted rather than man-powered, but it did manage flights up to 275 m (300 yards).

Two other MPAs (Man-Powered Aircraft) of the era were also launched with the aid of a length of rubber shock cord, and both were built for man-powered flight competitions. In 1933 Oskar Ursinus, editor of the German

One of the earliest protagonists of man-powered flight was the great polymath genius, Leonardo da Vinci. In this page from his notebooks is the sketched design for his 'Type E' semi-ornithopter. This was to have had its pilot in a hang-glider position, with fixed inner and flapping outer panels to the wings. The design dates from between 1497 and 1500. No indication is given of the mechanical linkage necessary between the pilot and the moving portions of the wings.

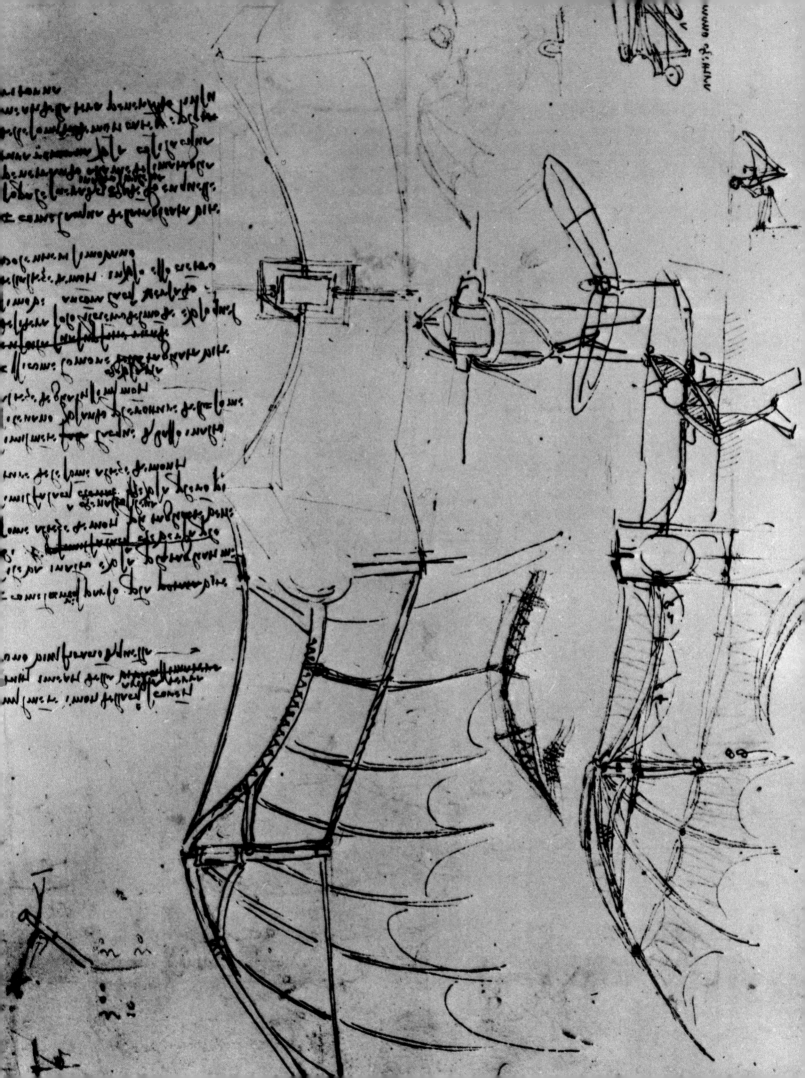

Flugsport magazine and sponsor of the *Wasserkuppe* soaring meetings in the Rhön mountains, put up a 500-mark prize for the first man-powered flight of 1 km (0.6 mile) around two pylons set 400 m (437 yards) apart, while the Italian government organized a similar contest.

Neither prize was won. Helmut Haessler and Franz Villinger, engineers from the Junkers company, built a sailplane-like aircraft called the *Mufli* which had a foot-cranked pusher propeller. It flew 722 m (790 yards) after an elastic-aided launch and was awarded a consolation prize by *Flugsport*.

Enea Bossi and Vittorio Bonomi's *Pedaliente* was bigger, with a wingspan of 17.6 m (57¾ ft) and had two chain-driven contra-rotating propellers. Thanks to the Italian government's asinine ruling that all MPA contestants had to conform to conventional airworthiness standards, the *Pedaliente* was far too heavy, weighing nearly 100 kg (220 lb), and could manage only downhill glides even after a bungee launch. The prize money remained firmly in the government's coffers.

Competitions seem to be the catalyst for man-powered flight; the Nazis even offered 5000 marks for a 500-m (547-yard) trip. Only a *Herr* Duennbeill tried for it, and failed. *Reichsmarschall* Hermann Goering awarded him a special Reich Leader of Air Sport prize for his trouble.

The real spur to the pedal plane movement came in 1959 at a time when man-powered flight was enjoying a revival in England. A millionaire industrialist named Henry Kremer promised £5000 to the first man who could pedal or otherwise propel an aircraft around a 1.6-km (1-mile) figure-of-eight course, crossing both start and finish lines at not less than 3.05 m (10 ft) above

ground. Kremer, a fitness fanatic who made his fortune from glassfibre plastics, imposed one other chauvinistic restriction: all claimants to his prize had to be citizens of the British Commonwealth, that increasingly small remnant of what used to be the British Empire.

The Kremer Prize

Enthusiasm ran high. The authoritative and influential Royal Aeronautical Society – the world's oldest aviation body – agreed to administer the competition and immediately appealed for British government aid to finance projects with potential, supported in Parliament by such politicians as Mr L. W. Teeling, Member for Brighton Pavilion, who spoke passionately in the House of Commons for the cause: 'There is a wonderful future for us,' he opined. 'I can well imagine, because of traffic, my Honourable

Friend the Parliamentary Secretary and I taking off in order to get here. We would have to get only just ten feet [3.05 m] in the air, just above the buses . . . no doubt every Member of Parliament would get extra votes by being seen at such a height.'

As ever, the lunatic fringe were quick to respond to Henry Kremer's offer. A Royal Air Force officer built a two-man pedal-driven helicopter which managed to rise 5 cm (2 in) before crashing back to earth. 'I still have a long way to go,' he told spectators superfluously. A Chelsea sculptor built a delicate, bird-shaped ornithopter which rose to 15 m (50 ft) on tow behind an automobile. A Londoner most inappropriately named Donald Partridge leapt off London's Hammersmith Bridge one foggy morning, flapping a pair of wings. He flew 15 m (50 ft) – straight down into the muddy River Thames, while in the north of England

another hopeless hopeful built a splendid helicopter in his garage, but was unable to persuade it to go through the doors. It may be there yet.

It was 1961 before significant flights were made solely by the physical effort of a human engine. The first was the Southampton Man-Powered AirCraft, SUMPAC for short, which was designed by students at Southampton University in the south of England. SUMPAC was of conventional sailplane appearance with a span of 24.4 m (80 ft) and an airframe constructed from spruce and balsa wood with parachute nylon covering. Its pusher propeller was driven by a twisted steel belt taking the drive from the rear cycle wheel. Derek Piggott, a well-known British glider pilot, was chosen to make SUMPAC's test flights. Piggott recalls:

'It was late in the evening of 9 November 1961, one of the most thrilling moments of my life. We had asked a cameraman to record what happened, we were that confident. It was damp and cold when I climbed into the seat and strapped myself in. The nose was bolted on. There was scarcely a breath of wind as I accelerated slowly down the main runway trying to keep straight . . . Pedalling the machine was rather like riding a tandem bicycle up a gradual slope with the girl friend not bothering to pedal. Then I eased back on the stick . . . the pedals began to slip a little and it all became easier. Tremendous excitement!'

Piggott was airborne. He flew about 45.7 m (50 yards) at a height of 1.8 m (6 ft). Subsequently SUMPAC made flights of nearly 805 m (880 yards), and the machine is now preserved at the Shuttleworth Trust Collection at Old Warden Aerodrome in England.

Hot on Piggott's pedals came employees of the de Havilland Aircraft Company, whose Puffin (so-named because it took a lot of puffin' to get it flying) flew a week later from Hatfield aerodrome. Puffin was slightly bigger than SUMPAC, with transparent Melinex covering and extreme dihedral on its 25.6-m (84-ft) wings. Its pilot, Jim Phillips, trained rigorously on a diet of steak and by the end of the year had flown the craft up to 686 m (750 ft) and made turns through 80 degrees. On 4 May 1962 Hatfield Man-Powered Aircraft Club chairman John Wimpenny flew the Puffin 908 m (993 yards). He was awarded a £50 prize for his record 805-m (880-yard) flight, which was not exceeded for ten years.

Continued failures

Mr Kremer's prize (raised to £10,000 and thrown open to all-comers in 1967) looked safe. The basic problem besetting MPA-builders was one of efficiency. At best the human body makes a poor powerplant: a 68-kg (150-lb) man producing a maximum of one half horsepower has a miserable

The SUMPAC may be regarded as the first man-powered aircraft to have achieved anything like a successful flight. The SUMPAC first took to the air on 9 November 1961, and was ultimately credited with a flight of 805 m (880 yards). Like other manpowered aircraft of the period, however, the main problem met by the designers and pilot was not flight as such, but the virtual impossibility of turning the aircraft in the air.

power-to-weight ratio, but one which is capable of sustaining flight provided the aircraft is very light (the Puffin, for example, tipped the scales at a scant 50 kg/110 lb), and has a high lift/drag ratio. Having achieved that, there are other problems. Because of their enormous wingspans, needed to provide the necessary wing area for ultra-low wing loadings, man-powered aircraft are difficult to fly accurately and have a tendency towards instability, which eventually proved disastrous to SUMPAC and the Puffin when their slow-responding controls failed to cope with gusts of wind.

The opening up of the Kremer competition to the world brought forth a great clattering of pedals from overseas, notably from Japan where Professor Hidemasa Kimura and students from the Nihon University in Tokyo embarked on a series of MPAs, one of which achieved a straight-line flight of 2095 m (2290 yards) in January 1977.

Back in Britain four more promising pedal planes had been financed by the Royal Aeronautical Society: Jupiter from Royal Air Force apprentices at Halton; Weybridge Group's massive Dumbo, which took 10,000 man-hours to build and had wings which spanned 36.6 m (120 ft) and drooped down at rest like a dying bird's; and the first two-man machines – Hertfordshire Pedal Aeronauts' Toucan (Toucan fly better than one) and the Southend Mayfly, which did not, as it was destroyed when a hangar collapsed.

Two human engines have thus far been the limit for MPAs, though scientists from the Canadian Aeronautics and Space Administration in Ottawa proposed a 56.4-m (185-ft) span machine called Cochkanoff which would have had a crew of seven, like some Roman galley of the air.

The Toucan was the first two-man craft to fly; in December 1972 it made a flight of 613 m (670 yards). Earlier in that year the Jupiter had broken the Puffin's decade-long record. It happened on a still evening in June, at RAF Benson in Oxfordshire. Piloted and pedalled by Flight Lieutenant John Potter, more usually to be found in the cockpit of a Hawker Hunter fighter, the Jupiter flew along Benson's runway in eerie silence for 1071 m (1171 yards), its slow-turning propeller beating the air like the wings of a bird, twilight reflected off the machine's silvery, iridescent Mylar covering so that it shimmered like a soap-bubble, soaring and dipping light as a leaf, moving in slow majesty like a vast mechanical dragonfly or a transparent-skinned tropical fish.

Splendid though the Jupiter's flight was, the Kremer Prize remained elusive as ever. The real difficulty was not so much the distance involved, but the requirement for a figure-of-eight course. Some disillusioned contestants thought it impossible, pointing

out that turning the long-winged machines through 180 degrees was like 'steering a bicycle with an 80-foot [24.4-m] pole lashed to the handlebars.' It was difficult to produce more than about five degrees of bank, even with full control deflections, and in turning flight the slower-travelling inner wing would cease to generate enough lift and start to drop. From a height of 3 to 4.6 m (10 to 15 ft) the crunch came quickly, and frequently. No wonder some grew disheartened; a rebuild might mean reassembling 12,000 fiddly parts. Such was the poor turning ability of the MPAs that the Jupiter's pilot, John Potter, estimated that a reversal of direction would require a radius of 3050 m (10,000 ft), and that the 1.6-km (1-mile) Kremer course would actually take 4.8 to 6.4 air km (3 to 4 air miles) to complete.

Even Henry Kremer himself began to wonder if he would live long enough to part with his money, so in a philanthropic gesture unparalleled in aviation history, he increased the reward to £50,000 and offered additional prizes for a flight around a slalom course and for a three-minute flight by a British entrant.

The 'Gossamer' concept

Thus far all the Kremer contestants had been pursuing the greatest possible aerodynamic efficiency, so that airframes were almost as complex, and often more obsessively streamlined than those of high-performance jets. In California, a professional meteorologist and former world champion sailplane pilot named Doctor Paul MacCready adopted a cruder, but ultimately successful approach. Starting with a paper napkin sketch (how many aircraft have been conceived on that humblest of plans, one wonders), MacCready calculated that a conventional hang glider weighing 25.6 kg (50 lb) needed three horsepower to fly. If the wing area was enlarged to 27.4 m (90 ft) while the airframe weight stayed constant, the craft ought to remain aloft on just one-third of one horsepower, a figure well within the capability of a trained athlete. During the summer of 1976 MacCready and his friend Doctor Peter Lissaman compressed years of aerodynamic research into computer read-outs to determine the best airfoils for efficiency operation at ultra-low airspeeds down to 8 kph (5 mph), a region which no-one had hitherto needed to investigate. What transpired from all that transistorized silicone-chip technology was a machine of (apparently) astonishing crudeness which spanned 26.8 m (88 ft) and weighed only 22.7 kg (50 lb). The entire structure consisted of a 5-cm (2-in) diameter aluminium wingspar with an outrigger-mounted foreplane or canard and a pusher propeller of 3.8-m (12½-ft) diameter. The framework was wire-braced and covered in ultra-thin transparent Mylar film.

Once the basic concept had been proved, a refined version called Gossamer Condor was built. The Condor spanned 29.25 m (96 ft), about the same as a Douglas DC-9 jet airliner, yet it weighed just 31.75 kg (70 lb) and had a wing loading of only 0.0176 kg/cm^2 (0.25 lb/sq ft). The DC-9, by comparison, has a wing loading of more than 7 kg/cm^2 (100 lb/sq ft). The wings were slightly swept back to aid stability, and the foreplane could be banked and its angle of incidence increased to start a turn, with the innermost wing warped to provide additional lift and thus balance the turn and prevent that damaging slip into the ground which had wrecked previous man-powered aircraft.

Bryan Allen, a racing cyclist and licensed pilot, spent four months working up physically for the assault on Kremer's purse. Allen could sustain 0.35 horsepower for 30 minutes, 0.45 horsepower for seven minutes, and could top 1.2 horsepower in short bursts; the combination of man and machine was near perfect.

Success at last

By the summer of 1977 the Gossamer Condor had made more than 430 flights and had accumulated more time in the air than all previous man-powered aircraft combined. Professor Kimura's balsa wood and rice-paper Stork had already doubled John Potter's record in Japan and time looked as if it might be running out both for MacCready and Henry Kremer's bank balance when Bryan Allen mounted the Gossamer Condor's saddle on 23 August 1977 for his 223rd flight. The wind at Shafter-Kern County Airport in California was a mild 3.9-kph (2.4-mph) zephyr as Allen lifted off and cruised for 152 m (500 ft) before clearing the 3.05-m (10-ft) T-bar marking the start of the course. Seven and a half minutes later Gossamer Condor landed back at the finish line after a perfect figure-of-eight flight, the slowest in aviation records, and probably the only one in which supporters have been able to run alongside shouting words of encouragement.

It seemed that the protracted race for man-powered flight was over, but then Henry Kremer stepped in with another £100,000, this time for the first man-powered flight across the English Channel. Smug aviation writers, including the author, were quick to laugh that one off; had it not taken 18 years for a man to pedal his way around a 1.6-km (1-mile) course? How many decades might it be before anyone could fly 34 km (21 miles), and over the windy, turbulent channel at that?

It took not a decade, not even two years, for all had reckoned without the obsessive determination of MacCready and his team.

In May 1979 an RAF Lockheed C-130 Hercules transport aircraft brought three new MPAs to England from California. These were Gossamer Albatrosses, very different from the Condor. The Albatross made extensive use of lightweight carbon-reinforced plastic in its structure, with wing ribs cut from expanded polystyrene foam, each weighing about 57 grammes (2 oz). Its 28.3-m (93-ft) wing could be broken down into four sections for ease of transport, and this time Allen had instruments – an airspeed sensor driven by a tiny propeller mounted on the foreplane bowsprit, and an 'altimeter' developed from the automatic focusing device of a Polaroid camera.

MacCready's major problems were no longer aerodynamic. The weather would play a major part in success or failure (hence the two spare aircraft), and the potentially disastrous effects of turbulence from passing ships (300 large ships traverse the Channel waters each day) could easily upset the low- and slow-flying Albatross.

The triumph of 'Gossamer Albatross'

'If the wind don't blow and the chain don't break...' proclaimed the MacCready team's T-shirts as they waited days, weeks for the right weather, which finally came with the dawn on Tuesday, 12 June. That morning a group of us were sitting in an office at the Paris Air Show, gazing out at the latest products of advanced aerospace technology when the telephone rang. 'He's done it!' said the lady from the US Embassy in Paris, 'Bryan Allen just cycled across the English Channel.'

Indeed he had, in 2 hours and 49 minutes, at an average speed of less than 13 kph (8 mph), the accompanying boat crews yelling altitude and airspeed advice to him when the batteries powering his instruments ran out, as did his drinking water. It seemed a truly magic achievement, coming almost exactly 70 years after Louis Blériot first flew an aircraft across *La Manche*.

Two days later they brought Gossamer Albatross to the air show, and hung her high in the *Musée de l'Air*, where the delicate, absurd-looking craft which spanned the width of the hangar yet weighed less than a child looked like some giant, nightmarish insect caught up in a web of roof girder braces. 'If you have any plans to mass produce the engine,' a Swedish girl told the shy Bryan Allen, 'I'd be very willing to help.'

They may mass produce the aircraft, though: having won the two major prizes for man-powered flight, Paul MacCready feels that the time has come to look at practical applications. The best chance, he thinks, would be as a mass-market sport-flying machine, which would sell for about £1000 and take about 200 hours to build.

With the Gossamer Albatross the man-powered aircraft may be said to have come of age. This aircraft, designed largely by Doctor Paul MacReady and Doctor Peter Lissaman, and flown by Bryan Allen, achieved the enormous goal of a man-powered flight across the English Channel on 12 June 1979.

Chapter 15

HOME GROWN

Since World War II aviation at virtually every level has become more expensive and increasingly hedged in by regulation. Yet many have felt the desire to fly in simple aircraft with little interference from the authorities, and this has led to a boom in the process of home-built aircraft, some of them possessing quite remarkable performances. Such aircraft can range from complex machines built from plans and kits, via an intermediate level of difficulty and cost, to the latest type of minimum aircraft capable only of limited performance, but costing little to make or run.

Above : The ultimate in home-built sophistication is represented by the jet-powered Bede BD-5J.

Left : The epitome of the 'fresh air' machine is the Breezy RLU-1, a three-seater with an open lattice-work fuselage, but with full flying instrumentation, radio and wheel brakes.

THERE WAS A time when a new aircraft design would start life as a hasty sketch on the flap of an envelope, the inspiration of one imaginative, creative mind. Modern aircraft are the brainchildren of service procurement boards and airline comptrollers, however: for any given role they will look much the same whether built in Long Beach or Leningrad.

Where then is there scope for originality and innovation, where can the fertile mind still be allowed to run riot? In basements, and backyards and garages, do-it-yourself homebuilders saw, hammer and rivet away on personal aircraft projects free of the constraints of multi-billion dollar development costs and capricious markets.

The idea that anyone, even without experience or engineering skill, could build his own aircraft gained credence thanks to a Frenchman named Henri Mignet, a self-taught amateur aircraft designer who created the infamous *Pou du Ciel* (properly translated 'sky louse', but more popularly rendered 'flying flea'), so named because Mignet said it was 'a small insect which made people scratch their heads'. Mignet's *Pou* and his book *Le Sport de l'Air* started a fanatical craze for do-it-yourself aircraft in the 1930s. 'It is not necessary to have any technical knowledge, if you can nail together a packing

case you can construct an aircraft,' he assured an eager and gullible public, many of whom were no great wizards with packing cases, either.

Flea fever swept France, Britain and America. In 1935 some 600 Flying Fleas were under construction in the British Isles alone, boosted by a national newspaper campaign to get the man in the street off the street and into the air. Most stayed firmly on the ground. Ignorant of the ways of aircraft, they built their Fleas too heavy, or used unsuitable engines, so that the machines would do little more than tear around refusing even to hop like their namesakes. It was a blessing in disguise, for the *Pou du Ciel* had an inherent design fault which killed 11 unlucky builders who did manage to get airborne. (One experienced British flier used to charge five shillings a time to test fly homebuilt Fleas, putting an absurdly low price on his life.) The trouble lay in Mignet's tandem-wing configuration: the rear wing was fixed while the incidence of front surface could be varied to give control in pitch. If the front wing was allowed to stall, the nose would drop and because of an obscure interference effect between the two wings the aircraft would dive ever steeper until it either became stabilized in an inverted position from which recovery was impossible, or struck the ground.

Above : The Mini-Mustang offered in plan form by Linn bears a fairly close resemblance to its celebrated forebear, seen in the background.

Left : Despite its venerable age, the plans of the Mignet *Pou du Ciel* are still sought, and amateur builders are producing their own variants on the Flying Flea theme with improvements such as modern engines, tricycle under-carriages and enclosed cockpits.

British Fleas were promptly grounded and most rotted away while their erstwhile constructors went back to packing cases and bookshelves, but Mignet fixed the problem and continued to build and develop *Poux* until his death in 1965. His dream of true amateur aviation, unfettered by regulation or supervision, died along with those unfortunate Flea fliers.

But one may still build a *Pou* today. Mignet's improved designs are still available, and other builders have updated the tandem-wing concept so that plans are on sale for a whole range of *Poux* from a tiny single-seater runabout to a six-place monster Flea used in France for dropping parachutists.

The homebuilt attraction

Why do people design and build their own flying machines? Part of the answer is that such a machine will likely be much cheaper than a purchased aircraft, provided one has the time to work on it: two years if one uses every minute of spare time, five if one intends to devote any time at all to other things. Then there is the satisfaction of being able to say 'I did it all myself'. But mostly it is because homebuilding is the only way to acquire original aircraft types not produced commercially.

Picture oneself as a World War I fighter ace: there are on the market plans and kits for full-size and scaled-down replicas of Fokker Triplanes, Sopwith Pups and Camels, SPADs and Nieuports, faultlessly reproduced with mock machine-guns which spit not lead but gas-cylinder generated muzzle flashes, fibreglass cowlings disguising their modern engines to look like castor-oil flinging rotaries.

A $100 set of plans can be one's passport to travel back in time to the open-cockpit, helmet-and-goggles days of *Hell's Angels*, or to the air war in Europe and the Pacific. An airworthy Supermarine Spitfire is a millionaire's machine, but English school-teacher John Isaacs has designed a six-tenths wooden scale replica of R. J. Mitchell's masterpiece, powered by a 100-hp engine so that those of modest means may act out their fantasies alongside the half-size Focke-Wulf Fw 190s, Mitsubishi Zeros, Republic Thunderbolts, North American Mustangs and Vought Corsairs offered by Californian company WAR Replicas. Their little fighters are built up from polyurethane foam and fibreglass over a basic wooden airframe. They have retractable landing gear and imitation guns, and without scale reference are uncannily like the real thing, all on converted 1600-cc Volkswagen automobile engines. Cost is in the region of $4000–7000, and 1500–3000 man hours to build.

Some people take this miniature air force

Possessed of futuristic lines, the Rutan Quickie is one of the latest designs for a home-built aircraft, and is a fascinating exercise in aerodynamic concepts, with great safety and a respectable performance.

thing to extremes. An American magazine once published a description of an imaginary scaled-down Boeing B-17 Flying Fortress which was supposed to fly on a quartet of lawn mower engines. They were inundated with calls from *Twelve O'Clock High* fans itching to start their own backyard 8th Air Force, begging for the plans. One was so annoyed on getting the joke that he swore he would go ahead and build the thing, just to show them, and he is apparently still at work on it.

Minimal aircraft

What if one wants something less ambitious? Three Americans named Charles Roloff, Robert Liposky and Carl Unger designed for fresh air fanatics an aircraft which they called Breezy. It is a most appropriate name, for Breezy's fuselage is nothing but an open framework steel-tube truss. There is no cockpit, or even a windshield for the pilot and two passengers, who sit open to the elements enjoying a view no other aircraft offers and which no-one who suffers from vertigo should try. Breezy uses the wings and tail surfaces from a Piper Super Cruiser, saving on building time, and looks like an aircraft someone forgot to cover; a ride in (or rather on) its girder-bridge fuselage is a chilly, draughty experience that is such fun it is difficult to stop oneself giggling foolishly, except when it rains, and it is virtually impossible not to wave at everything in sight.

Bud Evans's VP-1 Volksplane is another low-cost minimum aircraft which looks just like a rubber-band powered stick-and-tissue paper model, though it does at least have a rudimentary cockpit of sorts. The VP-1 is perhaps the closest modern equivalent to Henri Mignet's packing-case aircraft: its structure is all-wood, with plywood wing ribs which can be bulk-sawn from a stack of timber, and the engine comes again from the Volkswagen 'Beetle'. With 30 litres (6.6 Imperial gallons) of fuel and a standard-weight pilot aboard there is little room or payload available for more than a tooth-brush, but it flies, is cheap and quick to build, and one can tow it home behind a car with the wings detached. Thousands of Volksplanes are being glued together the world over; if they all get completed the roads (if not the skies) should be quieter without all those engineless VWs.

Not all homebuilt aircraft look like the boxes they came in. Given free rein over a pad of blank paper, designers have produced perfect, jewel-like creations of extraordinary sophistication which exhibit workmanship the like of which you rarely see on a mass-production aircraft.

Burt Rutan's Vari-Eze canard (*see Chapter 6*) is an example of original and effective thinking. Rutan has also created Quickie, a

most peculiar machine which looks like a sculptured, stylized dragonfly on the ground and a capital letter H in flight. Quickie is an ultralight powered by a 16-hp garden tractor engine. True to its name the prototype was designed and built in less than three months, scarcely an eye's blink in aircraft-building terms, and returns incredible performance figures for its minimal power: 201 kph (125 mph) cruise speed and 145 km (90 miles) on a single gallon of fuel. It has no tail surface, just a pair of sharply staggered wings with wheels set into the tips of the lower wing so that one can drive it around on the ground almost like an automobile without fear of scraping a wingtip. Quickie comes as a $4000 kit, complete down to the paint; just add 400 hours of work, say a year of weekends, and go flying.

Left: The Birdman TL-1A has the distinction of being the world's lightest powered aircraft, and is powered by a 15-hp McCulloch single-cylinder air-cooled engine.

Below: The Hovey Whing Ding is a simple biplane for home-builders interested in a low-performance 'fun' aircraft.

The ultimate homebuilt

For those who want more sophistication there is a homebuilt jet, the Bede BD-5J, dreamed up by entrepreneur and home-building guru Jim Bede as the ultimate toy for the man with everything. Bede accepted thousands of deposits on kits and plans for a propeller-driven version of the craft, and is now a tarnished hero among backyard builders still waiting for parts to finish their examples following Bede's financial collapse. The Bede BD-5J is powered by a 100-kg (202-lb) thrust Microturbo jet engine, spans just 5.18 m (17 ft), and is fully aerobatic. It is truly a dream machine among do-it-yourself projects.

For the family man looking for something different there is the Dyke Delta four-seat tourer, unusual in that it is both futuristically revolutionary and thoroughly practical, a perfect combination rarely achieved. The Delta's diamond-shaped wings fold for road-towing and garage hangaring, has a maximum speed of 306 kph (190 mph) and always draws an interested and enthusiastic crowd.

But let us go back to grass roots. The *raison d'être* of homebuilding has changed little since the Brazilian pioneer Alberto Santos Dumont built his little bamboo-framed *Demoiselle* in 1909 and threw open its design to anyone who cared to copy it. Santos's aircraft was an aerial runabout, a motorcycle of the air on which ordinary folk could go flying for the fun of it. Mignet's *Pou* had the same aim, and today there are latter-day Santos Dumonts and Mignets who may at last have made the breakthrough with cheap ultralight sport aircraft.

One such is the Birdman, listed by the *Guinness Book of Records* as the world's lightest rigid-wing powered aircraft at 54 kg (120 lb), and marketed by a Dayton Beach accountant who sells complete kits for less than $2000. The Birdman buzzes aloft on a 15-hp two-stroke engine, its pilot sitting out ahead of the wood and foam structure which is covered in a plastic heat shrink film used in radio-controlled model aircraft construction. Two gallons of fuel give it a range of 320 km (200 miles). Just a pound or two heavier is the Hovey Whing Ding biplane whose half-gallon fuel tank gives it a useful (their word) range of 16 km (10 miles). At least one is not likely to get lost away from base.

There is no limit to the creativity of home-builders. Amateur-constructed aircraft are the last bastion of the kind of original, albeit sometimes erroneous, design thinking which created the majority of the incredible flying machines in this book. Without the Flying Fleas, Breezies, Quickies and Volksplanes late twentieth-century aviation would be dull indeed.

INDEX

Picture credits

The publishers wish to thank the
following photographers and
organizations for their help with
illustrations for this book.

Air France Photo: 16/17
Avions Marcel Dassault: 91
BBC Hulton Picture Library:
  29, 32–37, 38, 92/93, 131
Bell Helicopter/Textron: 105,
  110/111, 113, 120/121
British Aerospace: 47, 53, 103
British Hovercraft Corp: 123,
  132/133
Canadair: 104
Don Dwiggins: 134/135
Du Pont (UK) Ltd: 2, 143
Fokker-FVW: 60/61
General Dynamics Corp: Front
  endpapers, 102, 130/131
Goodyear Tyre & Rubber Co:
  18/19, 26/27, 106/107, 108/109
Imperial War Museum: 40-45,
  51, 94/95, 116
Michael F. Jerram: 4–8, 12/13,
  16/17, 22/23, 30/31, 46/47,
  48, 56/57, 64/65, 67/68, 72–77,
  78, 81, 84–87, 90, 96/97,
  112/113, 114/115, 116–118,
  122/123, 126, 135, 138/139,
  144–146, 148–151
Kurt Lampart: 63
Lufthansa Photo: 128/129

Luftschiffbau Zeppelin GmbH:
  26
Mars: 12, 24/25, 90
McDonnell Douglas Corp:
  120/121
Dan Monroe: 2/3
North American Rockwell Corp:
  62/63
Northrop Corp: 52, 54/55
Novosti Press Agency: 89
Rolls-Royce (1971) Ltd: 102
Ryan Aeronautical: 107
Science Museum: 10, 14/15,
  20/21, 28/29, 37, 58/59
Shorts Aircraft Ltd: 98/99, 119,
  Back endpapers
Sikorski Aircraft Corp: 88/89,
  124/125, 127, 136
Summa Corporation, Nevada
  (print: Mars, London): 128/129
Talos Publishing Ltd: 101
John W. Underwood Collection:
  39, 77, 80, 82/83, 113, 146/147
University of Southampton:
  140/141
Vought Corp: 66/67, 70/71, 99
Westland Helicopters Ltd: 50